INTRODUCTION

It's often hard to articulate to others what I do as an Executive and Team Development Coach. It's a vague and varied job, this coaching role, and the industry is full of self-proclaimed coaches and consultants. Some of them are outstanding and incredibly talented. Some are not.

Here's what I'll say about coaches: Find one. Find a good one—someone who knows your business and who passionately cares about partnering with you to make you and your business better.

The best investment I have made in my life and in my career was to hire an executive coach. She is one of my blessings on earth, Jeaneen Schmidt. She's helped me to shine the light on my strengths, get out of my own way, and step into my life with such fierce courage that there is no turning back.

The process of writing a book has been completely against my grain. I have learned in my quest to improve myself and my business to self-assess my own talents and strengths and to discover where I resist following through on tasks such as this one. I am highly innovative, juggle many priorities at all times, and tend to do my best work under pressure—often at the last minute, when an important deadline is looming. (Some who know me might describe this process as "chaos," but it works for me.) Thus, one of my other coaches, my book coach, Patrick Snow, has held me accountable and given me deadlines. My book would still simply be an idea if not for him.

This book is an opportunity to take the most critical elements of my coaching program, "Managing for Performance," and share them with you. Here I will outline the key components of what I have learned working with great leaders, researching and studying what makes a great leader, and pulling together critical elements for building and maintaining a High Performance Team.

All of the stories in this book have inspired me to do what I do. It's always such an honor when one of my clients opens up his or her world to me and lets me in. I learn something every day from each of the amazing leaders and business owners with whom I work, so writing this book is my chance to share what I've learned. (My book coach has assured me that I can create as many revised and expanded editions of this book in the future as I wish, which is a good thing because I never stop learning.)

One final truth: There is no one right way to lead. But at the core of it all is knowing yourself at a deep level and having the courage to do what others won't do. Be authentic. Be willing to fail—a lot. And model for others what you expect them to be. If you can do these things, I think you can step into leadership and have a blast doing it.

I hope something in this work resonates for you. Skip through it and use what you can. Send me your thoughts via e-mail or on my Facebook Fan Page—I'd love to hear from you!

Theresa Callahan
tc@theresacallahan.com
Seattle, Washington
December 1, 2011

READERS RAVE ABOUT THERESA CALLAHAN AND *MANAGING FOR PERFORMANCE*

"Theresa Callahan has a wealth of experience and shares it via straightforward writing and engaging exercises. *Managing for Performance: Building Accountability for Team Success* is a practical and thought-provoking resource for both aspiring and seasoned leaders."

> **– Rick Carson**
> Author of *Taming Your Gremlin*
> www.TamingYourGremlin.com

"My definition of success is the Freedom to Be Yourself. Theresa Callahan's passion for honoring your instinctive talent and applying it to all that you do in life comes through in her book, Managing For Performance. Her innovative leadership coaching programs and straight-talk about the need to put the right players on the right team to enhance team success are right on."

> **– Kathy Kolbe**
> Author of Powered By Instinct and Pure Instinct
> www.Kolbe.com

"If you have ever met Theresa in person or had the privilege to do work with her, you would know that she has a strong dedication to the things that matter most in life: family, work, and clarity of mind. She listens and shares, is always available when she is needed, and always very present when she is with you. That these characteristics also come through in her writing is amazing. I highly recommend *Managing for Performance* if you want to live your life with purpose, passion, and performance. Theresa is an Executive Coach who lives her life with great intention, and she shares her passion for life with you in this book."

> **– Mark Demos, M.A.**
> Author of *LSI: The Forensics of Purpose, Passion and Performance*
> www.MyLifeScene.com

"Working with Theresa in partnership to build high performing teams has been a perfect fit for me! My personal belief is that everything you do and don't do affects others, and Theresa models this daily. She is passionate about her work as an Executive Coach and Teambuilding Consultant, and she strives for results in everything she does. *Managing for Performance* is filled with insights that will help anyone increase their results!"

– Marilyn Krichko
Author of *The Rowers' Code: A Business Parable of*
How to Pull Together as a Team—and Win!
www.RowersCode.com

"Theresa talks candidly about the challenges of creating a high producing team, and the difficulty that most business owners and team managers face when trying to hold their team members accountable. *Managing for Performance* is a powerful and engaging book that will be your toolkit for success as you take your role as a leader to the next level. Theresa provides personal stories of her experiences with her clients throughout the book that we can all relate to!"

– Patrick Snow
International Bestselling Author of *Creating Your Own Destiny* and
The Affluent Entrepreneur
www.PatrickSnow.com

"If you're in a leadership role, looking for inspiration, *Managing for Performance* is a must read. Theresa's stories about stepping up, taking ownership, and having the courage to get "un-stuck" will empower you to take bold action. The worksheets and activities in this book will help you create a high performing team with purpose and intention."

– Barbara Stanny
Author of Secrets of Six-Figure Women; Overcoming Underearning; and
Prince Charming Isn't Coming: How Women Get Smart About Money
www.BarbaraStanny.com

"Theresa has been and will continue to be a valuable resource in helping me select, train, review, and motivate my team. She has also been a true asset in consulting in other business management areas."

– Brady Nelson
State Farm Agent
www.BradyNelsonAgency.com

"Theresa is a highly successful professional sales coach and consultant. Her passion for excellence guides her work. And her tireless devotion to her clients keeps them coming back. Her sales experience and expertise provide the foundation for her practice, while her creativity and energy provide a memorable experience. Whether for a Fortune 500 company or an early stage start-up, a board of directors or a small sales team, Theresa can provide the right balance of learning and productivity. If you are looking for a high energy coach, and you want someone with the drive and professionalism to advance your company goals and objectives, Theresa is the perfect choice."

– **Bill Lawler**
Executive Vice-President of Sales
Sesame Communications

"Theresa is a terrific coach, consultant, and meeting facilitator. She delivered a thought-provoking working session on leading people through change and maximizing individual strengths for team success. I highly recommend Theresa as a coach, meeting facilitator, or business consultant."

– **Derek Jones**
Agency Field Executive
State Farm Insurance

"Theresa inspires greatness in every team she engages with. She is deeply committed to (and wildly successful at) creating transformation and success. Because she has walked her own path with courage and reflection, she is naturally able to call forth deep wisdom via her coaching and facilitation. If Theresa is crossing your path, know that she is bearing great gifts. Don't waiver. Say yes and receive them."

– **Jeaneen Schmidt**
Owner, J. R. Schmidt Coaching
www.JRScoaching.com

"Theresa is a breath of fresh air! She did a wonderful job for me in helping me utilize the Kolbe concepts to meet my staffing needs. She's very personable, upbeat, and passionate about what she does. It was a pleasure working with her and I look forward to using her coaching skills in the future."

– **Tim Butler**
Entrepreneur

"Theresa was fantastic to work with. She provided value to the many different personalities within the group and everyone gained from the experience. I would definitely work with Theresa again."

– **Carla Wigen**
Wealth Management Director
Wells Fargo Bank

"Theresa combined a really well-developed sense of what State Farm agents need to make their business work with the empathy to approach each agent as an individual. Her work made people's business lives better, which in turn made our customers' lives better."

– **Don Steiner**
Business Consultant and State Farm Agent

"We have used Theresa for over a year now with superior results. She has helped our group better understand one another and work more efficiently together in a manner that utilizes each member's unique talents and strengths. Theresa played a lead role in helping us hire new team members who are stellar fits for our organization and valued players in our group's future growth. We would wholeheartedly recommend Theresa to any organization looking to improve team efficiency and understanding."

– **Paul Grutzner**
Managing Partner, Clearpoint Financial
www.ClearPoint401k.com

"I hired Theresa to conduct a Kolbe workshop for my AFO team and for agents who chose to participate. She provided a very useful, applicable, and entertaining workshop that helped our teams to know: what our styles were and how we could work together most effectively, and what potential challenges we could face due to our different styles and strategies to overcome them. The workshop helped me better to allocate duties and to communicate my own style to work more effectively with my colleagues."

– **Laura Kunewa**
Insurance Vice President

A LEADERSHIP BLUEPRINT FOR HIGH ACHIEVEMENT

MANAGING
FOR PERFORMANCE

Building Accountability for Team Success

AVIVA
PUBLISHING
NEW YORK

THERESA CALLAHAN

ISBN: 978-1-935586-50-0

Library of Congress Control Number: 2012900161

Editor: Tyler Tichelaar

Cover Design: Lauri Cook, iMarc Consulting

Interior Layout: Fusion Creative Works, ww.fusioncw.com

Printed in the United States of America by DeHarts Media Services, Inc.

For additional copies, visit: www.TeamSynergyInstitute.com

To My Two Sons, Jackson and Wyatt

You inspire me to do what I do every day. This work and my passion for personal and professional development are fueled by both of you and by a desire to live a fulfilling life with you as you learn, prosper, and grow. You are amazing sons, great friends, funny, witty and talented individuals, and I learn from you daily. You make me laugh and bring me tears of joy and exhaustion—what a blessing I have been given to be your mom. I love you with all of my heart.

***

To My Mom, Joyce

Thank you for telling me I was a good writer when I was in 3rd grade, and for letting me remove the "h" from my name for a year in early elementary school when I learned how to pronounce "th" words. You have always inspired me to be who I am, and your encouraging words that I can be whatever I want to be when I grow up still resonate and echo with me daily. I think I have become exactly who and what I want to be in my life, Mom. My hope is that I just keep getting better at it. Thanks for always believing in me, no matter what. I love you so much.

***

To My Clients, My Friends, and My Followers

I do this work because you have called me forward to do it. It is such an honor to lead for you and with you. You have so much courage and you encourage me. May your dreams come true, and may you live your life with love and great intention.

ACKNOWLEDGMENTS

I just know I will leave out some important people here, but I need to thank a few people who have been instrumental in my professional and personal development. There are so many people who have affected and influenced me that I can't begin to list them all here! But I would like to give special thanks to a few people who have impacted my life. A few of these people do not know me or the impact they have made on my life. But most of you I know personally; you have taken a chance on me somewhere along the way or simply provided unconditional love and support to me in this journey. If not for you, this book and many of the blessings in my life would not be present.

The late Evelyn Brandl, Joyce Rickel, Steve Evans, Murvin Rickel, Chris Evans, Paula Evans, the late Robert Latrielle, Dave Barthelmus, the late Father Reedy, Ben Callahan, Kari Johnson Cullip, Jerry Woodahl, Nicole Spanovich Privett, Nancy and Bruce Callahan, Jack Barron, Ted Heaton, Dan Doran, Jim Skaggs, Mark Demos, Carol Flores, Tom Sessions, Lisa Shaw, Barb Brenner, Kathy Kolbe, Marcus Buckingham, the many leaders at The Coaches Training Institute, Jeaneen Schmidt,

Wayne Dyer, Susan Boelman, Susan Roser, Tracy Dieni, and Patrick Snow.

To all of you—thank you for the gentle whispers, the kicks in the butt, the straight talk, and the trust and belief in me. In some sort of way, I have received support from each of you and learned what it means to love, to lead, and to work hard to make my dreams come true. I am still listening and honored by your wisdom and teachings.

CONTENTS

CHAPTER ONE

STEPPING INTO LEADERSHIP

The task of the leader is to get his people from where they are to where they have not been.

~ Henry Kissinger

The development of your people is the most important role in running a business or leading a team. And it's interesting to me how surprised people are by the importance of this development once they arrive into leadership roles. Let's face it—some of us have arrived into a leadership role whether we are suited for the task or not! In my business, I have seen countless times where great salespeople were moved into management because they were great salespeople! "You're so great at selling stuff; let's move you into management so you can show other people how to sell stuff." But what if that great salesperson isn't a great leader? The two don't necessarily go hand-in-hand.

Some people are natural leaders; they seem to exude a magnetic energy and draw people to them with ease so others will follow. However, for most of us, leading with success requires some work. Talent in leadership, at its core, stems from artful and intentional practice and having a passion for wanting to bring out the best in others. Leadership is "other" focused, not so much self-driven.

I think Harvey Firestone, founder of Firestone Tires, said it best: "The growth and development of people is the highest calling of leadership." I believe Firestone was absolutely right. When you are called to lead, you are called to take your people where they have never been before. And sometimes that requires stepping out of the way so your people can step up.

One of my first leadership roles within an organization allowed me a great deal of flexibility and autonomy, but I still had to report to an executive. His job, as he described it to me, was to make sure I drove results, helped the agents with whom I was assigned to work to develop their businesses, and delivered the messages coming out of corporate so everyone was in alignment with company goals. He was skilled at letting me run with things, falling over the edge gently, and guiding me back on track as I stumbled through this journey of leading others. He was a master at letting me fall, watching me as I picked myself back up, and calling me into his office when I needed to be redirected.

One day, I came racing through the door of our management office, heading to my desk to prepare for my next appointment when I heard my boss, Jim, calling my name:

Boss: "Callahan, can I talk to you for a minute?"

Uh, oh. I always knew I had done something wrong when I heard that very quiet, slow, almost apologetic request to come into his office. (Jim's door was always open.)

Me: "Yes, boss?"

Boss: "Can you come in here for a minute?"

(He was always at his desk, thoughtfully working, reading reports, putting out fires over the phone, holding space for anyone at anytime to drop by and talk. He was counted on for always being available and listening.)

Me: "Sure. What's up?"

Boss: "You know that meeting we had on Friday with the agents and Dan?" (Dan was my area's Agency Vice-President at the time, the man who ultimately convinced me to leave being an agent and step into management. I adored him, and still do.)

Me: (pause) "Yes?" (I knew what was coming.)

Boss: You know, you aren't an agent anymore. You are a consultant to the agents. You need to let them talk. You need to sit quietly and listen, not question the leadership team when it is presenting to the agents. You are in management now. The agents are looking to you for guidance. They don't need you questioning the company's decisions.

(Before the entire group of agents, I had spoken up and challenged the Agency VP about an issue with one of our call centers. Not blurting out my thoughts was something I had never learned to do; it's something I've learned is one of my hard-wired traits, much to my pride and dismay.)

Boss: I don't like getting calls from Dan about things like this. I want to give you plenty of rope to run with things, to do what you want and need to do in your job, but there are times when I will need to pull the reins back a little to keep you out of trouble. Otherwise, I won't get in your way.

Me: Thanks, Jim. I'm sorry I embarrassed Dan. And I'm sorry I let you down. I won't let it happen again.

Boss: I know. That will be all.

When I returned to my office, I fell apart like a five-year old who had just been scolded by her father. I had let Jim down, and it cut me to the core.

Jim was an amazing leader. Quietly, and with great intent, I watched the people who reported to him strive to produce results because they wanted his praise. Jim innately understood that his role was to lead them, to let his team know he cared about them on a personal level (which he did and demonstrated daily). At district meetings, he didn't talk much, but when he did talk, everyone wanted to listen because he had something to say. He didn't candy-coat the tough messages; he didn't waste time getting to the bottom line. He was honest, candid, and told people straight up what he wanted and needed from them in order to achieve results.

In my organization, the Leadership Team was rewarded based on the results of the Agents. I have never seen a group of producers work so hard to achieve results so that the Leadership Team would "win." It was fascinating. Jim loved his people and they knew it, so they loved him. Jim held his team to being resourceful and talented individuals, and he knew they would do exactly what they needed to do if he would simply get out of their way and call them forward to step up to it. He provided guidance when he needed to, he was tough when he needed to be, and he recognized the good in others. And rather than strive to make changes in his people, he recognized them, often publicly, for their strengths and abilities and called them forward to do more—to do it better. He was a pretty simple man, not out to prove much to anyone. (In his early years, he'd had a great career as a professional football player for the Philadelphia Eagles so I guess he had already proven himself). But he was a man people wanted to know, gain the attention of, be associated with, and follow.

If you spend some time reflecting on the great leaders in your life, people you've lived with, worked with, learned about from others, you will probably find someone who has a vision and passion for bringing out the best in others, who is humbled by his or her own dream of making a difference, and who wants to leave a legacy—a path for others to follow.

I know what people will say about Jim after he's gone. I know the words that will be used to describe him. What trail do you wish to blaze in this journey called Leadership? What legacy do you strive to leave behind? What words will people use to describe you?

A very powerful activity I have done with my clients through my Leadership Development programs is an activity called "My Personal Mission Statement." It is a simple outline that allows you to think about the role you play in life and at work; it requests that you take a little time to think about the impact that you make. I ask now that you take some time to complete this activity and consider the impact you intend to make as a leader. Being in a leadership role, whether you are running your own business or leading a team, is not for the faint of heart. Take my challenge and spend some time writing your responses to the following questions.

PERSONAL MISSION STATEMENT

What would I really like to be and do in my life?

_____

_____

_____

_____

_____

What do I feel are my greatest strengths?

_____

_____

_____

_____

_____

How do I want to be remembered?

_____

_____

_____

_____

_____

Who is the one person who has made the greatest positive impact upon my life?

_____

_____

_____

_____

_____

What have been my happiest moments in life?

_____

_____

_____

_____

_____

If I had unlimited time and resources, what would I do?

_____

_____

_____

_____

_____

What are the three or four most important things to me?

_____

_____

_____

_____

_____

How can I best contribute to the world?

_____

_____

_____

_____

_____

_____

Your responses to this exercise aren't necessarily something you need to share with others, but if you do have a coach, a mentor, or someone you trust in a leadership position, I recommend creating a conversation around it with that person at your earliest opportunity. It will help you to create intention and purpose around why you do what you do every day, at work and at home, and ensure that you are living in alignment with your personal and professional goals.

You have been given the gift to lead and to create opportunities for others to step up. But you must have intention around your actions and your words so others can follow you with ease. Getting clear on your strengths, your talents, your purpose, and your personal vision isn't a luxury—it's a non-negotiable part of leading with excellence.

CHAPTER TWO

ASSESSING WHAT IS TRUE

"I think one of the greatest joys I have now in my career and in my profession is to be playing at an age where I can appreciate it more than I used to....It's a whole different lens you look through the older you get."
~Andre Agassi

In all things, we each have a unique lens we look through to assess what is true and what is, perhaps, imagined. Our experiences and where we come from mold who we are and how we see things. We wake up every day and see life through this unique lens that is our own.

Throughout my life, the people who care about me (and tease me) the most often refer to my rose-colored glasses. I ask that I please be buried in those imaginary glasses when my day comes because I do love them so. I take them with me everywhere I go. Sometimes they serve me well; sometimes they take me on a detour of avoidance. But I have had to learn over time that if I don't take the time every so often for a long and careful look in the mirror, I will not find the real truth. I have had to make such assessments in my personal life and in the development of my businesses. Assessing what is true is a vital piece of leading with authenticity. It isn't easy, and as I said in the first chapter, it isn't for the faint of heart. Sometimes, the truth hurts. And being a good leader requires talking about the tough stuff, just as much as celebrating the good.

In my quest to discover the truth, I have come to discover that I am *not* naturally great at everything! Yes, I have much room for improvement, and I learn on a daily basis where I need to balance out my wheel. Frankly, some days my ride is pretty bumpy, and I realize that without taking time to reassess how I'm doing in my business, just as in my life, I can go long stretches of time being "stuck" and feeling depleted because I'm either working against my grain or simply not paying attention to the areas of my life that need a check-up.

As a leader, it's necessary to allow yourself a check-up every once in a while. I'm not talking about performance reviews or feedback from the people to whom you directly report (if you have them); I'm talking about allowing yourself a good look at how your expectations and performance results are measuring up.

Generally speaking, I see my clients having great success in some areas, while barely holding on in others. This cycle can be exhausting because even when you are achieving results and desiring to celebrate your accomplishments, other areas in your business may be bogging you down and sucking the joy out of the good stuff until you feel like a kid holding a popped balloon.

We go to the doctor for annual checkups, we see the dentist regularly to get a fresh polish and make sure everything is going okay, and we set planning goals at work so we have a measuring stick by which to determine whether we are on track for results. But how often do we assess, as leaders, how well we are doing in the key areas of our business development? I'm talking about an intensive look at how balanced we are in all areas of leading our team.

You can set goals and even produce powerful action plans to achieve them, but if the systems and processes of your organization, its infrastructure, are not in place, you will feel like you are rowing upstream without a paddle. Being in that position is exhausting; when the business can't do what it's trying to do, it affects the bottom line and depletes your resources.

Let me give you an example:

I have a client in the retirement planning industry who is breaking records and achieving wild success as his business explodes with growth. He is a very talented and passionate man who is on the edge of some great developments in his field, gaining recognition and notoriety for his accomplishments. His business is flourishing. He is making money! People are writing about him, and he is on his way to fame in the industry. Wow! Sounds like he's got it all figured out, doesn't it?

The thing is, his clients' demands have exceeded his ability to service their needs! He is growing and has a great need for adding talent to his team, but he is now in a very reactive state of needing to hire yesterday. He is now searching for talent in such a frenzied state that it feels like an overwhelming task. Additionally, the systems and processes in his office just don't work anymore—everything needs to be revamped!

"Didn't he see this coming?" you might ask. Well, sure. But he has been in the trenches working so hard to respond to everything that has been going on around him, that he hasn't had time to focus on the organizing and staffing part of the business! So, here we are, in what should be a time of excitement with so much to celebrate, instead in a bit of a reactive crisis mode. The main task his team is facing is ramping up the systems, processes, job descriptions, and staffing in hopes of getting back on track. The physiological effect this situation has on his team members is overwhelming. They are exhausted, cranky, frustrated, depleted.

I have no doubt that this team will get back on track. But this situation is an important reminder that we must constantly look at all of the elements that play a role in intentional business development in order to keep things running smoothly. An occasional bump in the road is expected as you lead a team to new levels of success, but one of the most critical roles in leading a team is to take inventory regularly on how smooth the ride is for everyone, paying close attention to those areas that need your immediate and direct attention.

As an Executive Coach and leadership consultant, I have fully integrated some foundational work that has made a big impact in helping my clients to gain clarity about where they are having ease at work, and where they are feeling "stuck." I have found that my clients often know where they are stuck, generally speaking, but they are so overwhelmed about feeling held captive by the weight of this stuck place that they don't know how to get out. That is often where I step in.

Through my work and studies at The Coaches Training Institute, I have adopted and modified some powerful tools that have served to be transformational for my clients. Among them is something that is called the "Leadership Wheel." I am going to walk you through this process, allowing you an opportunity to self-assess how balanced your wheel is as a leader.

This exercise is adapted from *Co-Active Coaching: Changing Business, Transforming Lives* by Henry Kimsey-House, Karen Kimsey-House, and Phil Sandahl. (This book has been the foundation for much of my coaching work so I recommend it to anyone who leads and coaches others.)

In the exercise on the following page, you will have an opportunity to self-assess your level of satisfaction about how well you are doing in eight critical areas of your business development as the team leader. I believe these eight areas are vital to leading a team to success.

LEADERSHIP WHEEL

Directions: Score (0 low to 10 high) your satisfaction with your ability in the following areas:

Planning and Budgeting: establishing detailed steps and timetables to achieve results and then allocating the resources necessary to make them happen.

Promoting Stability and Order: creating the potential to produce consistent key results through systems and processes that honor the business' needs.

Motivating and Inspiring: energizing people to overcome major political, bureaucratic, and resource barriers that prevent change by satisfying basic, but often unfulfilled, human needs.

Aligning People: communicating, by words and deeds, the direction needed to achieve progress and success; it must be communicated to everyone whose cooperation may be needed to create a team that understands the vision and strategies and accepts their validity.

Establishing Direction: developing a vision of the future, often the distant future, and strategies for producing the changes needed to achieve that vision.

Promoting Change: creating the potential of producing useful change (such as desired new products or shifting the organization's culture).

Controlling and Problem-Solving: monitoring results in detail, indentifying deviation from the plan, and then organizing to solve these problems.

Organizing and Staffing: establishing a structure for accomplishing plan requirements, staffing that structure with the right people, delegating authority for carrying out the plan, providing policies and procedures to guide people, and creating methods of systems to monitor implementation.

LEADERSHIP WHEEL

The eight sections of the Wheel represent Balance. Seeing the center of the wheel as 0 and the outer edges at 10, <u>rank your level of satisfaction</u> with each area by drawing a straight or curved line to create a new outer edge. The new perimeter represents the wheel of your life as the Entrepreneur and Leader of your business. If this were a real wheel, how bumpy would the ride be?

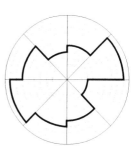

Sample Chart

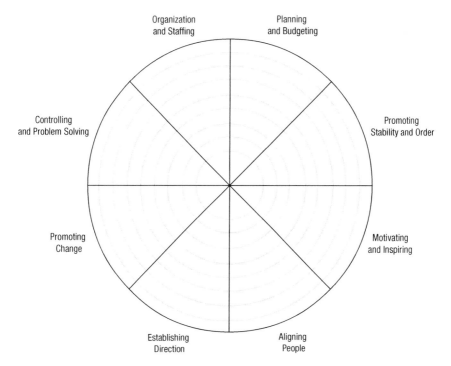

Check in:

What did you discover about your Wheel? Is it a smooth ride for you and your team right now? Are the bumps so big that it feels as if you are falling into a road construction pit?

This exercise is an opportunity to look at where your team is having ease, success, and synergy. The visual diagram you have created will provide you and your team feedback that your efforts are moving you forward. Take time to tell your team what you are noticing in regards to its success and how each team member contributes to the smooth ride—that acknowledgment can produce powerful results in keeping the good stuff going!

This exercise also allows you some powerful insight into where you are feeling "stuck" as team leader. If you scored any of the areas in the 4-6 range, you know you have some work to do. And, in my experience, if you scored any of the areas at a 3 or lower, you are in or near a crisis— red alert!—your business needs you now! Now you know what areas of your leadership and team development need immediate and urgent attention. Call your team members together to see what they think. As a leader, your job isn't to figure it all out; it's your role to shine the light on areas that need your attention and to call your team forward to figure it out with you.[1]

Important Note: Holding your team members to the goals of being creative and resourceful by asking them to problem-solve with you is a powerful form of leadership. You don't have to go it alone. If you did, why have a team? The most effective leaders I work with call their teams forward on a regular basis to enroll them in creating change. Our team members will come up with ideas we might never even think of! And there is nothing more exciting than watching team members commit to a problem-solving task with renewed energy. They see things we, as leaders, cannot see because they are on the frontline. Brainstorm and

---

1 In the following chapter, you will begin to spend more focused attention on the areas of the wheel that require the most attention. Refer to thecoaches.com for updated assessment tools and resources.

strategize with them every opportunity you have and let go of the idea that you have to be the one always to figure it out.

Isn't it enough for you to keep your team members on track and provide the feedback they need to do their job with excellence? And isn't it a wonderful gift to you, as leader, not to have to do it alone?

The fun of leadership is only just beginning!

CHAPTER THREE

SETTING INTENTIONS

Our intention creates our reality.
~ Wayne Dyer

In leadership, just as in life, it isn't enough just to want something to happen—we have to be willing to get into the trenches to make it happen. And without setting intentions to make something happen, ideas, thoughts, and words will just sit there and float through the air like dust. The particles of brilliance will disappear with the wind and no execution will be seen.

Good leadership requires doing things that others won't do. It's about taking action and having the courage to stand up for what you believe is true, even when it goes against conventional wisdom. As John Quincy Adams, our sixth U.S. President, so eloquently put it back when he was a leader of our country, "If your actions inspire others to dream more, learn more, do more and become more, you are a leader."

President Adams was only in office for one term; he didn't have the popularity to be re-elected, losing to President Andrew Jackson. However, as an American diplomat and a man bred into leadership, he was a bold and courageous man. His efforts did a lot to change the country and move it toward progress. As a diplomat, he helped to develop America's foreign policy. And even after he left the office of the president, he remained in Congress, advocating for the end of slavery until he died at his desk in 1848. Now, that is leadership and dedication. He certainly left a trail for others to follow by paving the way for other great leaders in American history.

It has been said that when you are a leader "it's lonely at the top." And, for some leaders, this statement might be true. However, setting intentions and then executing the actions *with your team* to make change or to inspire others is what sets the excellent leaders apart from all others. Who says leadership has to be a lonely place? What if you thought of it as being more like a dinner party where you are simply the host?

Take a minute now to reflect back on the first exercise you completed in this book, your Personal Mission Statement, from Chapter 1. What was it about this exercise that stood out for you? When you think about the question, "How do I want to be remembered?" what comes to mind? It's a powerful question. It's an important question. It allows you to set a course of intention that serves as a platform for all of your current and future decisions to be made, personally and professionally.

I do a lot of work with entrepreneurs and small business owners. I am especially attracted to this group of people because entrepreneurs have a certain spirit that fascinates me. These are people who are willing to take risks and try things differently. They are so courageous! And they have a vision and a dream for creating a good life for themselves, their families, their clients, and the world. They want to leave a path for others to follow. They want to leave a legacy. And I believe they want to control their own destinies.

I had the privilege several years ago to spend a week at the Gallup Institute as part of a certification training program for using an assessment tool that helped to uncover traits and characteristics of high performing team members within my organization. It was fun and interesting work, especially since I have followed the leaders within the Gallup Institute for years. In this program, we discovered that people who spend a lot of time thinking about their family and their career are more likely to act on a goal-driven basis. Their values and beliefs are in alignment with their work, and they are intentional about creating purpose in their work.

Since that time, I continue to follow the brilliant work that comes from Gallup. One of the most popular books that has flown off the shelves of bookstores around the world is *Well Being—The Five Essential Elements* by Tom Rath and Jim Harter, both published best-selling authors and pioneers at Gallup. In their research, Roth and Harter write that "Wellbeing is about the combination of our love for what we do each day, the quality of our relationships, the security of our finances, the vibrancy of our physical health, and the pride we take in what we have contributed to our community. Most importantly, it's about how these five elements *interact*."

Guess what is the #1 Element of Wellbeing—Career Wellbeing! Roth and Harter open the first section of their book by asking, "Do you like what you do each day?" How many people can genuinely answer "Yes" to this question?

What if you, as a leader, could influence this response for everyone on your team so it is a "Yes"? Well, guess what? YOU CAN!

Our career wellbeing is so important on so many levels. It defines who we are and what we do every day. And this comes as no surprise, if you think about it. What is the first question you ask people when you meet them for the first time?

"What do you do?"

Crafting a job that brings you happiness and a sense of gratification is what I call a non-negotiable for getting it right when it comes to leading people. And without clear intentions about who you are and where you intend to go, how can you expect to get there?

Creating intention, in all leadership concepts, requires the creation of a roadmap for your success. This process doesn't have to be lofty or difficult, but it does require, as I so candidly say to my clients on a regular basis, having a talk with yourself.

What do you love to do? What are you great at? How can you do more of those things on a daily basis so you have joy and ease in your work, which naturally leads to success and increased productivity?

And where do you get "stuck"? My clients will hear me ask this question over and over again through our working partnership because the process of rebalancing will never end as long as you are a part of the team. Taking inventory is vital because it allows you to set intentions and plans for making dreams and goals a reality.

For many years, I've known a client, Dave, and for the past year, I've been actively in the trenches with him, assessing team talent, rewriting job descriptions, setting goals, implementing accountability measurement tools, and integrating new systems and processes for increased efficiency.

Dave has owned his business for over thirty years. Around the time of his business' thirty-year anniversary, he invited me to lunch. I was curious about what was going on with Dave, and I assumed he wanted me to help him with his business development, but because we hadn't talked for a while, I suspected there might be more going on. Here are the highlights of our conversation over pasta on a Thursday afternoon:

Dave: Theresa, I'm about to celebrate thirty years in my business. I can't believe it's been thirty years.

Me: Wow, Dave! Congratulations! This is a celebration! Wait, you aren't thinking about retiring are you?

Dave: Well, no. But, Theresa, (with this chin and face resting heavily in his hands as his arms propped him up on the lunch table), something's gotta change. Some days, and I even hate to say this out loud, I just don't like going to my office. I hate feeling that way, but if I'm going to keep doing this, I think I need to make some changes.

Me: I hear what you are saying, Dave. And you know what? If you decided to leave today, no one would be surprised—I mean thirty years is a long time in this business, and you are an excellent business man. You are on the top of your game. You've accomplished a lot.

Dave: Ya, I suppose, (looking around the room and leaning in to whisper with great expression) but I'm not done yet!

(Dave's eyes widened with anticipation. Dave looked like a cat that had just swallowed a mouse. No one was going to take this opportunity from him and he was NOT done.)

Me: (laughing and settling into the overstuffed chair) Dave, I can see that. Good for you. This is exciting! How can I help you?

By the end of our conversation, Dave and I had designed a coaching agreement to begin some intensive work together. We did transformational work with his team during that time. And when that contracted ended, he renewed his contract with me for another three months to ensure the systems and processes we created were fully integrated.

Through the process of coaching Dave, the most powerful thing I experienced was witnessing him step into a new business leadership role. He knew that if he was going to stay in his role as the leader of his business, he needed to make a change. He knew he needed to make sure that he had the right people in the right jobs, that they knew what was expected of them, and that they were held accountable for achieving their goals. Dave wanted me to partner with him to get him to that place, and it has been an honor for me to watch him recommit to his business with such passionate intent.

At one point during our working partnership, while a lot of team transformation was taking place, Dave brought his wife (who's been a supportive, impactful, and silent business partner through all of these years), his daughter (who currently acts as office manager to the business) and his son-in-law (who recently joined the team to drive new production growth) to one of our coaching sessions. During this ninety-minute, in person session, we talked collectively about the roles and responsibilities each of them had, at home and at work, in driving their business forward. They'd all decided to throw their proverbial "eggs" into this "basket"—the family business—at least for now, with great gusto, and they wanted to get it right. And they were all driven to create results. The courage and vulnerability it took for Dave and his family to open up their world to me in this way overwhelmed me.

This level of dedication, this process of getting clear on what's working well and where the team is "stuck," allowed Dave to set about his strategic business planning in a way he has never done before.

Dave's not done yet. He's a leader among his peers, a leading producer in his zone, and a leader to everyone who knows him. He has pride knowing he has helped to build his company, and he considers it an honor to serve his clients. I know he will never stop learning or asking questions. He has a vision of excellence, and I don't believe much will get in the way of that vision. I will always be on Dave's team—I predict that we will e-mail, talk, and collaborate for many years to come.

Will Dave leave a legacy? You bet he will. Does his community know who he is? Of course they do. And will Dave still have days that are exhausting, frustrating, and challenging for him? YES!

But what Dave has modelled for all who know him is a new approach to living his life and running his business: He's doing it with Intention. And it is a beautiful thing to see.

In this next activity, you will be given the opportunity to set intentions for yourself and for your team.

PRIMARY FOCUS

Refer back to the Leadership Wheel Exercise in Chapter 2. I'd like you to pick three areas on the wheel to assess. In the space below, name and describe the three areas you would like to hold as the primary focus of your leadership development. For each area, provide a simple heading and a sense of where you currently are feeling "stuck."

EXAMPLE: <u>Planning and Budgeting</u>

"I have been running my business for almost 8 years now, and I am tired of feeling like my overhead is out of control. I don't want to continue relying on my line of credit and personal assets to pay my bills at work – I want my business to pay for itself."

1._____

_____

_____

_____

_____

2._____

_____

_____

_____

_____

3._____

_____

_____

_____

_____

Now, for each item that you wrote down, I'd like you describe what it would look like if it were a "10."

In other words, if you ranked yourself a "3" in the area of "Planning and Budgeting," I'd like you to describe what a "10" would look like.

Example:

<u>A "10" in Planning and Budgeting will require:</u>

- Having a budget in place that allows me to prioritize spending and saving for the bottom line.

- Knowing what my overhead is and honoring my budget on a monthly basis.

- Making sure the bills are paid on a timely basis and that forecasting is seamless.

- Having a marketing budget in place that is in alignment with our production goals.

1. A "10" in _____ will require:

- _____
- _____
- _____
- _____

2. A "10" in _____ will require:

- _____
- _____
- _____
- _____

3. A "10" in _____ will require:

- _____
- _____
- _____
- _____

EXECUTING FOR RESULTS

Once you have identified the three primary areas you want to focus on in your leadership development, you can create goals to help you achieve results. I don't recommend tackling more than three goals at a time. The idea here is to stay focused on what Franklin Covey so brilliantly describes as the "Wildly Important Goals." Too many goals will overwhelm you and prevent you from staying focused.

Using the Action Plan Worksheet on the next couple of pages, list three goals to focus your efforts during the specified period. The goals should be challenging, but realistic, specific, measurable, and within your control.

GOAL PLANNING WORKSHEET

Goal #1

Determine the timeframe: quarterly, yearly

Goal #1 _____

Special skills/knowledge/strengths I can use to reach this goal:

_____

_____

_____

_____

What motivation do I have to accomplish this goal?

_____

_____

_____

_____

Steps to achieve this goal:

- _____

- _____

- _____

- _____

How will I know when I have achieved this goal? (What accountability measures are in place to track results?)

_____

_____

_____

_____

Goal #2

Determine the timeframe: quarterly, yearly

Goal #2 _____

Special skills/knowledge/strengths I can use to reach this goal:

_____

_____

_____

_____

What motivation do I have to accomplish this goal?

_____

_____

_____

_____

Steps to achieve this goal:

- _____

- _____

- _____

- _____

How will I know when I have achieved this goal? (What accountability measures are in place to track results?)

_____

_____

_____

_____

Goal #3

Determine the timeframe: quarterly, yearly

Goal #3 _____

Special skills/knowledge/strengths I can use to reach this goal:

_____

_____

_____

_____

What motivation do I have to accomplish this goal?

_____

_____

_____

_____

Steps to achieve this goal:

- _____

- _____

- _____

- _____

How will I know when I have achieved this goal? (What accountability measures are in place to track results?)

_____

_____

_____

_____

CHAPTER FOUR

ACCOUNTABILITY FOR ACTION: ESSENTIAL BEHAVIORS OF LEADERS

The leader must be in charge of getting things done by running the three core processes—picking other leaders, setting the strategic direction, and conducting operations. These actions are the substance of execution, and leaders cannot delegate them regardless of the size of the organization.

~ Ram Charan

DEVELOPING YOUR PEOPLE

If you aren't empowering your employees, if you're not calling them forward to greatness, and if you're not recognizing them…you're missing the opportunity to make your organization great.

Finding talent within your organization and "shining a light" on those talented individuals so they can inspire others is a vital part of leading and developing your people.

To me, it's about ownership. As leaders, sometimes we have to get out of the way so our people can step in and lead with us. If we don't give our team members a chance to step up and step into their greatness, they will never have a chance to show us what they have to bring to the table.

But what about those who don't step up when we call them forward? Well, that's another important discovery that we need to make, right? Sometimes people don't want the ownership we desire them to have. And we might as well find that out early on in the working relationship. My philosophy is this: Step up or scoot over. Because we've got a business to run here.

I do a lot of work with my clients on rebalancing team talent. I find the greatest experiences are always a result of getting the team members involved in the process so they will take ownership for the day-to-day business operation.

The most powerful way I have found to increase ownership on the job is to co-create job descriptions with the team members that will fit their talents, their strengths, and their interests. When a team member has an opportunity to create his or her job, work is easier, more fun, and more gratifying, and that all results in increased productivity.

The easiest way to co-create to increase job ownership is to meet with your individual team members one-on-one to discuss their roles and responsibilities. During the conversation, be sure to ask these simple questions:

What are you good at that you also love to do at work?

Where do you get "stuck"? What are those things you know you aren't good at and don't enjoy doing at work?

These questions are powerful because they get right down to the basics of strengths and weaknesses—we all know what we are good at and where we find fulfillment in our work, and we also know where we fall short and get sucked of our mental energy to perform tasks we either aren't suited for or simply don't enjoy. When we have the freedom to say out loud what we like and don't like, what we are good at and what we are not, it allows for open dialogue about where we excel and where we feel held back.

Once the truth has been told and we are given permission to talk about these things, creative energy can take over as we fine-tune job descriptions, roles, and responsibilities. Renewed commitment can happen with long-time employees who have seemed apathetic or unmotivated when they have an opportunity to renegotiate the terms! It's fascinating to watch a seemingly unengaged employee kick it into gear as he crafts his new job description built entirely around the things he knows he is good at and loves to do. And will this employee leave? Not anytime soon!

Hand-in-hand with fine-tuning job descriptions is making sure that each employee has a professional development plan that supports his or her roles and responsibilities! If someone is going to take on new challenges, let him help to design the training, education, and professional coursework he needs to achieve excellence.

Tal Ben-Shahar, Ph.D. and lecturer at Harvard University, talks a lot about the connection between emotional involvement with our work and high performance. In his book, *Happier*, Beh-Shahar says, "Because we often perform best at the things we find most engaging, pursuing those activities that provide us meaning and pleasure could actually lead to more quantifiable success in the long run."

We all only have a certain amount of mental and physical energy to expend every day. Why not direct that energy in a way that is natural, and easy, and FUN? (I'm a big believer in having fun at work. It's okay to have fun at work.)

As I said earlier, the great thing is, you, as "boss," as the leader, don't have to figure this stuff out alone. When your team members get involved in their personal and professional development and have a voice in the destiny of their career path, you add a multiplier on the effectiveness and overall wellbeing of your people. It's worth it to get this part right. And you don't have to do it alone. This is about ownership – the ultimate fuel behind productivity!

DIRECTING YOUR PEOPLE

Rebalancing team talent never ends. And once you have the right people in the right spot, paddling in motion with everyone else on the team, things begin to happen.

A great example of directing your team is in setting clear goals: Measurable and specific goals for which everyone feels ownership. But what is the point of crafting goals and action plans to achieve them if there is no follow-up and accountability to ensure the goals are reached? And what happens when the non-doers don't do what they said they would?

Without clear goals and expectations, it's hard for people to succeed. And it's a complete waste of everyone's time if you are going to set goals and let people quietly just fall short without consequence and redirection.

I recently met with one of my clients, whom I'll call Joe. He called me because he has been frustrated lately about the lack of production his team has performed. We decided to meet for coffee at a spot near his office. Here is how our conversation went:

Joe: Theresa, I'm really frustrated because I like my people, but they just aren't doing what I need them to do. We are falling behind in production, and frankly, I can't afford to keep them all onboard at the rate we are going. We are losing business and not writing enough new business to replace those accounts, so I don't know what to do.

Me: Sounds like this is keeping you up at night, Joe. I can imagine what a worry it has been. What needs to happen?

Joe: Well, I need my people to step up a little, and just do what they said they'd do.

Me: Joe, do all of your team members have defined job descriptions with goals for their roles in running the business?

Joe: Huh? You know, a few years ago we had some, but we haven't really looked at them in a while.

Me: I see. So how do your team members know what is expected of them?

Joe: Well, our business is pretty busy. We just take care of our clients when they come in or call—it seems like we are all busy and doing the best we can.

Me: So, most days you're simply showing up and faced with a lot of activity, requiring you just to respond to everything that is going on? Is that what typically happens for everyone in your day at the office?

Joe: Yes. Unfortunately, when I hear you say it like that, that's the reality. I mean, we do meet once in awhile for team meetings, but those are usually just to share announcements or talk about issues people are having. Those meetings are good, but we don't have them as often as I'd like.

Me: It sounds like everyone would benefit from some strategic planning—a chance to review their job descriptions and create some structure around why they do what they do every day. I mean, it's hard to achieve results when you aren't even really clear on what's expected of you. And if everyone is in a state of reacting to the chaos that is going on all around you all day, that is likely exhausting and frustrating for everyone. What do you think?

Joe: I think you are right. What should I do?

Me: Let's start by asking what the business needs from your team, Joe. And then we can sit down with the team and some blank sheets of paper to work together on some solutions to get you where you want to go. If your team members are committed, and they want to help you gain control of business productivity, they will step up. But you need to show them how they can help.

Joe was relieved and encouraged that he could get the team on track by stepping back and taking a long and thoughtful look at what the business needs from him, as leader, and from the team members, as the engine that drives his productivity.

Regaining clarity on how everyone can contribute is the first step in redirecting your team to high performance. You, as leader, have to step in and model this piece of creating change. Start by taking a close look at what your personal contribution is to the team, and remember that the biggest hat you wear is that of managing and leading your team. It takes patience, curiosity, and a whole lot of intention to get the team back on course, and it's 100 percent up to you to make it happen.

Important Note: Not all great leaders are made overnight. Get clear on what you can do yourself, as leader of your team, and where you need support. Surround yourself with partners who can help you get where you need to go. Enroll colleagues who are great at it, hire a coach, and reach out for help. And if you need to hire someone to help you with the Human Resources part of running your business, do it.

MANAGING THE BUSINESS FOR YOUR PEOPLE

At least once a day, in conversation with my clients, I can be heard saying, "Honor your business."

What I mean by that is: Whether you're a business manager or business owner, it's your responsibility to pay thoughtful and constant attention to the needs of your business in order to achieve results. If you don't do it, who will?

Your business needs you to be the strategic leader. And that requires making tough decisions about the systems and processes of getting things done. It demands that you keep your finger on the business' pulse on a daily basis. And it requires that you continually keep a bird's-eye view on the overall business needs.

And here's the biggest deal of all: If you aren't taking care of the business, and the business falls short, you will never be able to take care of your people. You see, they are counting on you to get it right. If the business' needs are not being honored, and the business fails to achieve the desired results, no one on the team will truly be able to feel like he or she is part of something great.

To be a strategic leader, it's necessary to get out of the business' day-to-day operations. It's hard to get a meta-view, to see the big picture, of what your business needs when you are stuck in the chaos of activity.

Stephen Covey, whom I think is one of the best thought leaders on business management, has done some interesting work on what he calls "getting caught in the whirlwind; being suffocated by the activities of the day job." Being caught in that whirlwind will prevent you from being able to be the strategic leader of your business. "When you lose to the whirlwind," says Covey, "it is your fault. And there are rules for executing in the face of the whirlwind. Four of them, to be exact."

Covey states what these are in his book, which I encourage you to read, *The 4 Disciplines of Execution*™:

Discipline 1—Focus on the wildly important (goals)

Discipline 2—Create a compelling scoreboard

Discipline 3—Translate lofty goals into specific actions

Discipline 4—Hold each other accountable—all of the time

Setting goals is nothing new. But how often have you set goals only to find them sitting on the counter months later, with no execution? I think the important element here is to focus on what I call the "non-negotiables." What are those things that *have* to happen in order to achieve results? Start simple and don't lose focus on the most important goals for your business.

Having a "scoreboard" is critical! I love seeing teams that have visual display boards in the office that everyone can see. If you don't track your results and make it clear what the target is, how will you ever know when you get there!? We work hard every day to achieve results, so make sure everyone knows where you are at all times.

I think what Covey is talking about when he refers to "lofty goals" is taking ideas and making them realities. Breaking things down to specific action steps that are doable will be the only way you achieve results with ease. Who's doing what, when, and how? This part of execution is one the entire team can influence—collaboratively. As strategic leader, you might have to deliver your company's objectives and show your team how you are going to track results. But getting the team involved in the action steps to achieve those results takes the accountability game to a whole new level. Getting the team together to strategize is a great way to spend a day or a half-day off campus where you won't be disturbed, and a great way to strengthen team alliance!

Lack of accountability is the #1 thing that holds us back as teams. Goals, tracking systems, and action plans won't get us anywhere if we aren't holding each other accountable all of the time. If you want buy-in from your team members, ask them to create accountability measures with you. Remember, there is no one right way to do this!

Final Thoughts on Leading for Results

I have become acquainted with a talented man named David Evans, a retired award-winning leader in the Hospitality Industry. David was senior Vice President of Marketing and Global Sales for Westin and Starwood resorts and is a member of the Hospitality Sales & Marketing Association International Hall of Fame. He says his thirty-nine years of service and leadership in his industry taught him about what he has coined as the "Four P's" of great leadership:

#1: Product

#2: People

#3: Process

#4: Profit

"To be a great leader, you need the Four P's," David says. "You need a good product, good people, a good process, and profit. But you can't focus on #4 until you have focused on all the others."

I love David's laser focus on these critical elements for getting it right as a leader. And he has reminded me of many other conversations I have had regarding leadership: You have to believe in your product, have people whose talents and values are in alignment with your business, and have systems and processes in place that will allow everyone to thrive. Without these things, you will not achieve profitability. At least not for the long-haul.

Great leaders need to have extraordinary vision and a laser focus on the business objectives in order to achieve extraordinary results. And, as I have learned in my training for running half-marathons, there is no shortcut in getting there. You have to invest the time and the hard work into training to get there. But crossing that finish line (your goals!) with your team is the most rewarding experience you can achieve. So let's get you there.

CHAPTER FIVE

WHAT DOES IT MEAN TO HOLD MY TEAM AND MYSELF ACCOUNTABLE?

It is not only what we do, but also what we do not do,
for which we are accountable.

~ Moliere

I have a client in Alaska who runs a great business. She has been in business for almost twenty years and has a team she truly loves. They work together, they socialize together, they laugh together, and they seem to enjoy each other's company.

During an off-site study group meeting, where I was a speaker, this client sat quietly for some time when the topic of Accountability came up. This group of high-achieving women was talking about how frustrating it is when your team members don't follow through and do the things they are expected to do.

Suddenly, my client spoke up. Here is what she said:

Client: You know what really makes me mad? My lead salesperson, who has been working in my office with me for over ten years, has a problem with showing up for work on time. I mean, our phones start ringing at

9:00 a.m., and sometimes she's not even in her seat until 9:15! It drives me crazy!

Me: Yes, that would make me mad, too. How are you handling that?

Client: Well, I'm not sure what to do. I mean, the office opens at 9:00 a.m. She should be there at 9:00. I said something to her about it a while ago, but she either forgot or just doesn't care that it bothers me.

Me: Either way, it seems that she doesn't respect the rules of the office. And that's a big deal. But an even bigger deal is the message you are sending to everyone else on the team when you let her get away with that. How do you think it's affecting everyone else?

Client: Oh. (long pause) I guess I hadn't really thought about that.

Me: You know, if being on time by having the butts in the chairs at 9:00 a.m. ready to go is the expectation, then she needs to be there at 9:00 a.m. with her butt in the chair ready to go. It's not fair if everyone else on the team follows through on that commitment and she doesn't. You are sending a loud message to everyone else on the team by doing nothing about it when she is so boldly not honoring your office rules. Is this your intent?

Client: No. You are right. I will have a talk with her when I get home. I feel terrible; I never realized how much this problem affected everyone.

My client loves her team. She wants to maintain a friendly relationship with each of her employees, but she wants them to respect her. Setting standards, following them, and expecting everyone on the team also to follow them is a part of modeling what you want your team members to do and who you want them to be.

When accountability measures are not in place, it's hard to expect action. In fact, I'd say that it's a waste of your time and resources to hold planning events and create action plans if you don't intend to follow through. Talking about ideas, making plans, and dreaming of possibilities can build camaraderie and bring people together for brainstorming and team building purposes, but without accountability measures in place to track your progress, you have very little chance of meeting your goals.

At its core, **accountability is the responsibility to act**. It is the commitment to do the right thing and to stand by your decisions. I have found that this quality comes from within; ultimately, the individual must hold himself to the highest standard first. Without accountability, it is almost impossible to achieve outstanding results throughout the organization.

In a recent Harris Poll, 2.5 million people were surveyed on the effectiveness of their organization and their managers. Only 10 percent felt their organizations held them accountable for results.

Those who manage by accountability also know that accountability is a quality that can be developed, honed through practice, and encouraged in others. Leaders who have a management philosophy of personal accountability also seem naturally to model the qualities of integrity and responsibility for their organization. It's an easy act to follow for a committed team.

In his best-selling book, *The Five Dysfunctions of a Team*, business consultant and speaker Patrick Lencioni describes the many pitfalls that teams face in their development. This book explores the fundamental causes of organizational politics and team failure.

The five dysfunctions the author highlights are:

- Inattention to Results

- Avoidance of Accountability

- Lack of Commitment

- Fear of Conflict

- Absence of Trust

Instead, Lencioni states that these very dysfunctions should be turned around to become the building blocks of the team to achieve the following pyramid of results:

If we know trust is the foundation for all teams, and all relationships, we can start from that place. But we still have to be authentic and be willing to talk about the hard stuff when things aren't going well.

Lencioni says, "The need to avoid interpersonal discomfort prevents team members from holding one another accountable for their behaviors and performance."

What I think is so vital about Lencioni's theory is that if we can't manage conflict, how can we move toward results? What I see happen on many teams is an innate need for the team leader to create affiliation among his or her team members. There is often a perceived conflict that arises when we have to abandon our role as the "nice guy" to be the "bad guy" (the boss) and enforce the rules! And the smaller the team, the more chronic the problem.

I would go so far as to say that avoiding conflict and enforcing accountability is worse than having no accountability measurements in place at all. Does that sound harsh?

Let me give you an example:

Last year I designed and facilitated an off-site planning event for a business team in New Jersey. Following our off-site event, I offered to conduct some follow-up work to assist with the integration of some of the concepts that we introduced at the meeting.

In this business owner's office, the phones ring off the hook from morning until closing time and throughout the weekend, even when the office is closed. Currently, eight people are on this team. I have visions of them all sprinting through the office some days in reaction to their clients' needs.

Since our off-site meeting, I have had approximately six phone calls that were either missed or rescheduled due to last minute "emergencies." It is chaos in the office. Yes, they are busy and they are writing a lot of new business, but they are in such a frenzied state most days that it's a wonder to me they don't collapse at each day's end.

This client has been difficult to coach. He is losing money due to his inefficiencies. I also recently learned that this office is losing clients to competitors at about the same pace that they are writing new business. In the insurance business this situation is called a "lapse/cancellation ratio." It's vital to keep that ratio as low as possible, meaning to write substantially more new business than you lose, if you are to run an efficient and profitable company.

My work with this team has proven to me yet again the importance of having in place:

1. Systems and processes (the business infrastructure)

2. Clearly defined roles and responsibilities

3. Accountability measures to keep the business on track

This business is losing the company money. Its employees are operating in a responsive mode on a daily basis, as opposed to being proactive and working with intention.

Not surprisingly, this team has seen a team member turnover of nearly 100 percent in the past couple of years. Am I worried about the existing team members sticking around for a while? You bet I am. Am I worried about this team's wellbeing? Of course I am!

The off-site meeting that this business owner invested in was a fun team-building opportunity to get away from the office and play together, as well as get to know each other better on a personal level, but when the team leaders do not put accountability measures in place to integrate their work fully, we can predict what will happen when it's time to evaluate results: Failure.

Lencioni notes that another vital element of the avoidance of account-ability is the role of the leader to confront difficult situations. And "without commitment to a clearly defined set of goals, team members will hesitate to call their colleagues on their actions and behaviors that are counterproductive for the team."

Set goals for your team as a team. Do it together whenever possible. And honor them. It's even okay to change the goals when you need to redirect your course, but have them and make sure there are structures in place to remind everyone on a daily basis where the target is. Make sure everyone knows who's responsible for what and that accountability measurements are in place to track your results regularly.

Roll up your sleeves and take your team with you. And those who don't follow you need to find somewhere else to work.

Enough said about accountability. For now.

CHAPTER SIX

TEAM TALENT AS IT RELATES TO HIGH PERFORMANCE

A really great talent finds its happiness in execution.
~ Johann Wolfgang von Goethe

If there is one thing a leader cannot negotiate in the development of his or her team, it is Team Talent. The greatest resource you will ever have in the development of your business is your Human Capital. You've got to get this one right.

There is ***nothing***—no amount of money, no bonus program, no incentive pay, nor any training program—that will match having the right person in the right job.

I could dedicate this entire book to this topic. In fact, so much reading material is out there on this subject that it could make your head spin. So, I'm not going to spend time here repeating what you've already read or telling you something you already know. However, I assume if you've made it to this section of the book (and some of you might have skipped right to it at the moment you opened the book), then you probably are experiencing the same thing every other business owner and team leader

I ever worked with is experiencing: The greatest challenge of developing your team is hiring, training, and retaining good talent.

I meet so many people who are unhappy, dissatisfied, or who are still trying to figure out what they are going to be when they grow up. It's as if they are doing their time, waiting to see what's next, hoping that something will shift, and then suddenly, someday they will wake up and be in the career of their dreams!

In my practice, I have done a lot of Career Coaching. Sometimes my clients don't even realize that their career is what they are being coached on, but every time we step into the conversation about having the freedom to do what you are good at and what you like to do, you are re-evaluating your job.

Here's the deal: You are the only one who will get in the way of achieving what you want to achieve in your career. And if you are in a leadership position, you have been given the powerful gift and good fortune to be able to help others discover their innate talents and strengths so they can create a job that is the perfect fit for them.

A couple of years ago, I learned about the popular lecturer, Tal Ben-Shahar, whom I mentioned earlier in this book. He is a professor at Harvard University who teaches a class on positive psychology. Thousands of students have lined up for a chance to get into his classes; in fact, approximately 20 percent of all Harvard graduates have taken his course. I have recommended his book, *Happier*, on countless occasions, and I travel everywhere with it. The bright yellow book cover catches the eye of my audience whenever I speak at events, and inevitably, I get into conversations about the book's content on a regular basis.

Happier has an entire section dedicated to happiness in the workplace. And it comes as no surprise that the section's premise emphasizes the need for each of us to find meaning and purpose in our work.

Dr. Ben-Shahar sums it up best when he says, "We naturally work harder at the things that we care about and are interested in—that we are passionate about. For a person experiencing his work as a calling, work is an end in itself."

When you have the freedom to do what you do best at work every day, work is gratifying. It's fun! And productivity soars through the roof when these elements are in alignment.

All of us only have a certain amount of mental and physical energy to expend. And when that energy is used up, we begin to check out. It isn't until we've had a chance to refuel and replenish that we can come back with energy to be productive and get back on track with our work.

When you reach that point of depletion on a regular basis, especially in the workplace, it's easy to see how some people produce poor results, don't reach goals, get cranky, call in late, spend too much time in the bathroom…you know where I'm going with this. Working against your grain is exhausting, mentally and physically, and costs the company a LOT of money.

As a Kolbe Certified™ Consultant, I have had the great fortune to learn about some fascinating research that brain scientists have been doing with the Kolbe Corp, based in Phoenix, Arizona. Kathy Kolbe, an internationally known conation theorist, has been assessing behaviors related to conation for over thirty years with a wide variety of subjects from around the globe.

Kolbe and Pierre Balthazard, professor at Arizona State University and an acknowledged expert in the brain activity of leaders, recently released preliminary results of a study of conation in the brains of community leaders. "Conation" is the part of mental life that has to do with a desire to strive based upon one's own volition.

Balthazard, whose work is funded by the Defense Advanced Research Projects Agency (DARPA), analyzed the subjects using qEEG brain signal processing techniques. The study was supported by research partners including the Arizona Science Center, Banner Health, the EDGE Innovation Network, and Valley Leadership. The initial findings of the theorists' research show that the brain works far more efficiently when it has the freedom to perform a task according to its natural conative patterns of action—the person's unique modus operandi, or M.O.

In an October 2010, press release,[1] Kolbe stated, "This (research) supports my theory that conation is the one human factor that gives us equality as well as our unique character….You can manage your response to a situation, but your M.O. is made up of strengths that are hard-wired Action Modes in your brain." In the same press release, Dr. Balthazard noted, "Previous brain research looked primarily at things that weren't working well. Researchers studied disabilities and brain injuries….By learning from healthy brains of high performing people, we've learned lessons that could be applicable to a broader population."

This powerful research validates that having the right people in the right jobs is not only important from a Career Wellness perspective, but that you can suck the resources of an organization dry in a blink of an eye when you are expending mental energy from your people in an ineffi-

1 http://www.kolbe.com/pdfassets/BrainResearchPressRelease_10-6-10.pdf
The trademarks listed are the trademarks of Kathy Kolbe and Kolbe Corp

cient way. It isn't simply a luxury to match the "fit" with the job; it actually costs the organization money every day that you don't get it right.

I have witnessed the physiological effects of having the right person in the wrong job. I have seen people get sick, physically, as a result of working against their grain.

I have a wall hanging in the entry of my house that says, "This isn't a dress rehearsal. You might as well be happy." I love this phrase because it's so true! What's the point of being unhappy at work? And why hold employees back by letting them stay in jobs where they are unhappy, unproductive, not reaching goals, and sucking the wind out of your business?

If you have team members whose talents are not suited for the job, HELP THEM TO LEAVE! Assist them on getting clear about what their talents are and let them go—set them free so they can be happy and create a career that is better matched for them. Everyone will thank you in the end.

HONORING THE BUSINESS' NEEDS

Time and time again I've seen great leaders expend countless hours stressing about keeping an unproductive team member on board just because the person is "so nice." They don't want to fire this person because they think, if given just one more or three more or many more chances, the person will turn things around and start producing the results he or she was hired to do.

WRONG!

When you have the right person in the right job, and that person has a clear job description that outlines his roles and responsibilities, and he has the freedom to do his job, he will naturally produce results! Ongoing coaching and accountability meetings will ensure that you are both in alignment with the tasks at hand and the results being generated, but it shouldn't take that much energy to get the job done!

Sure, things come up that get the entire team off track at times, but if your people are in the right place and there are systems to support them, it should be easy to regain focus and carry on with ease when the bump in the road has passed.

What does the business need from the team? If you haven't taken time to assess the business' needs, it will continue to be a struggle for you to develop team talent.

Pull out your business plan. Take a look at the size of your business, where it is, and where you want to take it. From this place, get whatever help you can to assess your organization's needs from a talent perspective.

If top-notch customer service is one of your goals, then determine how many people you need in place to tend to your clients' needs.

If business growth is a top priority, fine-tune your sales team's job descriptions to determine whether you have the right people in those sales jobs. If you don't, and you need to hire new, or more, talent—market the job for that position!

The biggest mistake I have seen my clients make is trying to make the person fit the job. Popeye said it best when he proclaimed, "I Yam What I Yam!" If you continue trying to make people do things they are not naturally suited to do, you are sure to fail. And keeping your head buried in the sand month after month, holding your breath, and "hoping" for a change in results is just postponing the inevitable fact that your employee will, indeed, eventually leave. And what a terrible feeling for that employee to be in a job he knows he is not suited for. Have the courage to put everyone out of his or her misery by honoring the person and honoring the business. Being "nice" isn't useful. Being kind is. And sometimes the kind thing to do is to help someone to move on to what is next in his life, while simultaneously honoring your business' needs.

CHAPTER SEVEN

RECRUITING, ONBOARDING, AND RETAINING TALENT FOR HIGH PERFORMANCE

What do the best college sports teams do? Recruit the best players all the time! When a business is short-staffed, that is the worst time to recruit because you are desperate. It is much better to recruit and network all the time, so the pipeline is full when you need it. Just like college sports teams, when you recruit the best you get a reputation for excellence and great players (employees) want to be on your team. Recruiting gets a whole lot easier when you have a reputation for being a great place to work.

~ Joanna Meiseles

This past year, I launched my newest client service: Team Member Recruiting. This has been a dynamic and necessary part of my team development work and a result of my clients' pleading for help and my colleagues' brilliant support. As luck would have it, I was surrounded by talented recruiters and passionate business owners who helped me build the Team Synergy Recruiting model. Launching this new service just made sense.

Here's what I'm learning: The stakes are high when you're recruiting. The industry rule of thumb is: the wrong person costs you three times his or her annual salary. A $50,000 employee costs you $150,000; a

$150,000 employee costs $450,000. That's for starters. There's also lost opportunity cost…plus lost business, potential customers, and momentum. And you're back to square one, looking for a replacement.

Do these estimates seem unusually high? Consider all of the factors that affect your bottom line when you've hired the wrong person:

ACTUAL AND HIDDEN COSTS TO HIRING THE WRONG PERSON

DURING HIRING PROCESS

- Recruiting Fees

- Resume screening

- Interviewing Time/Expenses

- Advertising/Marketing Materials

- Testing

- Assessments

- Reference Checks Time

- Background and Credit Checks

- Medical Exams/Drug Tests

DURING TRAINING AND EMPLOYMENT

- Relocation Expenses

- Temporary/Contract Employment Fees

- Employee Benefits

- Licensing fees

- Orientation Materials

- Lower/Lost productivity during training time

- Training Programs

- Emotional Stress on Manager/Co-workers from frustration of working with the wrong person

- Payment for sick days and overtime for other employees when wrong employee doesn't show up for work.

AFTER LETTING THE WRONG PERSON GO

- Lower/Lost Productivity during Interim among Managers, Coworkers

- All of the Above Hiring Costs Again

- Increased Unemployment Taxes

- Time Spent Fighting Terminated Employee Unemployment Cases

- Separation Processing

- Separation Pay

- Accrued Vacation

- Continued Benefits

- Potential Loss of Intellectual Property

- Loss of Physical Company Property including keys, uniforms etc.

- Changing the locks on the doors

- Lower Morale from Overwork

- "Chain Reaction" Turnover

- Client Issues from Turnover

- Client Loss

- Emotional Stress on Manager and Co-workers from coping with the situation

INVESTING IN TEAM TALENT AND MAKING SURE YOU GET IT RIGHT

Team Synergy Recruiting was launched as a result of several of my clients requesting help to get talent! They reported a high level of exhaustion and frustration at making poor hiring decisions and really needed help. And I realized, in my holistic approach to the team development part of my work, that recruiting good talent was the missing link in helping my clients create high performing teams. When I am brought into an organization to focus on leadership development, teambuilding, and business planning, a lot of emphasis is put on making sure we have the right people on the team.

I believe your talent is the engine that drives your business productivity. When team talent is missing, it holds everyone back. But finding the right "fit" is only just the beginning.

What makes our recruiting program unique is the consultative approach to the recruiting process. This concept isn't about putting warm bodies in front of business owners for interviews, *hoping* for a good "fit." It's about honoring the business' needs, crafting job descriptions that clearly define job roles and responsibilities, creating a strong pool of candidates to fill those needs, and providing tools and resources for a strategic onboarding process once the new hire starts the job. By "strategic onboarding" I mean the process by which you integrate the new employee with the team. And even more than that, to bring a new employee onboard in a strategic manner means that you sell that employee right away on the business and its goals to make sure he or she will be a key team player and enjoy working for the business. The end result is a new hire whose talent and strengths perfectly match the business' needs—a really great start to a team member affecting the organization's bottom line productivity—and a custom-designed process for helping the team rebalance.

During the years I have spent running my own businesses and coaching other entrepreneurs and leaders, I have discovered what I believe are Ten Key Elements for recruiting, onboarding, and retaining talent.

TEN KEY ELEMENTS FOR RECRUITING, TRAINING, AND RETAINING TALENT

Key #1: Identify what the business needs.

1. Assess team talent—ask, "What's missing?"

2. Rebalance—"Reforming" a team means opportunities for everyone!

3. Ask, "What does the business need?"

Have fun taking inventory on what the business really needs, and don't forget to GET YOUR TEAM INVOLVED in this process! Together, you can craft a job description that will honor the business' needs so you can start the recruiting process.

When the team works together to craft the job descriptions based on the business' needs, then engagement and commitment from everyone increases. (Always a great situation for the boss!)

Key #2: Create job descriptions that include the job's key characteristics.

The job description might seem basic and obvious, but a clear job description for everyone on the team is necessary if you want to achieve results.

Start by making sure the team members have clearly defined job descriptions that highlight their individual contributions to the business. In bullet format, have each employee work with you by listing out the specific tasks he or she manages, oversees, or performs every day to drive productivity.

Once each team member is clear on his or her and everyone else's roles and responsibilities, you can begin crafting a job description for your potential new hire! Working together on this process makes the job easier for you as team leader, and it's empowering for the team members.

It's easier to meet expectations when those expectations are clear. And updating job descriptions on a regular basis is an important element for keeping your good people on track.

Key #3: Take inventory on your product—your business.

1. Is your business marketable?

2. Are there systems and processes in place to bring onboard new talent?

Candidates who are looking for a new career and a great place to work need to know that your business will be a perfect fit for them. What do you have to offer top talent that can't be found at your competitors' place of business? Why should the individual come to work for YOU? Get clear on your business' features and the benefits of working there—you have a lot to gain by recruiting the best talent, so make your business the best choice for that individual and market your opportunity well.

Making an offer and closing the deal is only the beginning of hiring top talent. And "the honeymoon phase" of a new hire ends quickly, so be sure a comprehensive onboarding process is in place to acclimate new employees and immediately provide them with the professional development they will need to be successful. If your business environment isn't set up for added talent and an orientation and training program isn't in place to support new employees, you will face retention problems down the road.

Key #4: Recruit talent that fits the job—no negotiating.

Recruiting top talent requires matching the "job" with the "talent." So why do so many people end up in a job that doesn't "fit"?

If you've ever had a job you didn't like, or you weren't good at, you know what it means to "work against your grain." And how long is someone willing to work against his grain? Not very!

No amount of money, no incentive program, and no benefits package is more valuable than being in the RIGHT job! In fact, the most successful people I meet proclaim that they have jobs they LOVE: They get to wake up every day and go to work to do what they are **good** at!

It has been proven, and I have witnessed this fact over and over with my clients, that we naturally work harder at the things we care about and we are interested in, at the things we are passionate about and are naturally good at.

In *Wellbeing: The Five Essential Elements,* authors Tom Rath and Jim Harter share vital research about the elements we all need to achieve wellbeing in our lives. Guess what the #1 Element listed is? You got it: Career Wellbeing. And it's no surprise—what's the first thing you ask someone when you meet him: "What do YOU do?"

We all need to find purpose in our work in order to achieve success, naturally. "People who have the opportunity to use their strengths are six times as likely to be engaged in their jobs and more than three times as likely to report having an excellent quality of life," according to Rath and Harter's research.

We all know how expensive it is to hire the *wrong* person. What we tend to forget, as hiring managers, is that it is also mentally and physically draining to ask someone to work against his grain—to do things he is not suited for and simply not good at.

Find talent-based assessment tools to measure your candidate's talent and use strategic interview processes to help your people get it right. Honor the business' needs to determine what talent the business requires, and then be strategic in your recruiting efforts to ensure you fit the talent with the job: I promise you will see increased results and improved employee satisfaction, which has more intrinsic value than anything you can "pay" your people.

Key #5: If it's a sales job, the new hire needs to show up ready to sell (licenses acquired, etc.)

In many professional industries, the sales team needs required licenses to sell and consult clients about the products and services the business offers.

Interestingly, I am hearing more and more from my clients how their salespeople "can't pass the licensing tests" or are "taking too long to get licensed" in their first few months on the job.

I have a problem with this situation. I mean, if it's a sales job, and the job requires a license to legally sell the products offered, shouldn't the person be licensed on his or her first day of work?

Here's a tip: Tell your new hires to get all of their required licenses BEFORE they show up for their first day of work. Let them know you will reimburse them for their licensing expenses, if you are willing to do that, in their first paycheck.

If your new hire is committed, he will have no problem fulfilling this requirement. And he will be able to hit the ground running and make bonuses and commissions on his first day on the job.

Key #6: Have a 90-day onboarding process that includes an orientation program and accountability measures.

The first 90 days on the job are vital. In this time, the new hire needs to learn deeply about the culture of the organization and what roles and responsibilities he will have. This time should focus on these key areas:

1. An orientation process. If there is an employee handbook, the new hire should get a copy or spend time reviewing it with the team

manager. It should be clear how things are managed in the office, what the office policies are, how things like vacation and sick days are handled, and general processes that need to be followed. This time is also an opportunity for the new hire to find out who the organization's key players are and whom to go to for what. A training plan should be put in place with the new hire, and action plans for his or her onboarding process should be communicated.

2. A 30-, 60-, and 90-day review process. Taking time to sit down with your new hire at 30 days allows for a check in from all parties to talk about how things are going so far. Keep it simple and seek feedback on how your new hire is doing from his or her point of view. Sample questions during a one-hour meeting might include: "How are things going for you so far?" "What's working well?" and "Where do you need more support?" This meeting is also an opportunity for you to provide specific feedback on what you are noticing with your new employee, such as where he is excelling naturally and where he seems to need help getting acclimated. If specific Action Plan items were established during the hiring process, now is a wonderful time to review how the new hire is doing by achieving goals. It is imperative that you provide feedback and document your conversation. Setting action plans for the next 30 days allows you both to set goals for ongoing development and training, and it allows you something to measure at the 60- and 90-day review.

The 60-day review allows you to deepen the conversation from the 30-day review and track progress. Ask the same questions you did at the 30-day review to make sure you and your new hire are still in alignment. Make sure your new employee is being provided with adequate training so he or she can excel quickly. Look for signs of his being self-motivated and committed to the new job. And continue tracking results with ongoing action items for improvement.

By the time the 90-day review rolls around, you now should know without a doubt whether your new hire is going to make it long-term or not. I have many clients who make a permanent offer of employment at this 90-day review, with increased earning opportunity, benefits packages available, and a full integration of employment. You need to be sure a contract is in place to support this process if this is your approach, but it can be very intentional and powerful for both parties when everyone knows the first 90 days is a "trial" for permanent employment.

The bottom line in the 90-day onboarding process is this: You want to be certain your new hire will bring to your business the value you are investing your time and talent in to achieve. As we know, the honeymoon phase ends quickly with a new hire, and it is a wonderful gift for everyone on the team when this initial working relationship comes with a system for success. It's expensive, monetarily and emotionally, to hire the wrong person. So having systems in place to support the business during that first 90 days will help you to hire with ease and ensure your new hire is fully committed before you permanently commit to each other.

A sample Employee Performance Review is in the Resources section in the back of this book for your use.

Key #7: Co-create an ongoing professional development plan with the new hire during the first 90 days.

During the first week on the job, you will be able to determine immediately where the new hire needs the most training and development. Putting a plan in place now for the first 90 days allows you and the other players on the team a strategic opportunity to get the new team member up and running quickly. It also allows you another opportunity for measuring the new hire's development from an accountability standpoint.

Creating a plan for the first 90 days also allows you an opportunity to talk about your new employee's future goals and what kind of development plans you will need down the road. This conversation is especially vital if you are hiring someone who will move into a bigger role at some point in the future or who aspires to be a leader for your organization.

Ultimately, you will see your most talented team members striving continuously to learn and grow. Because we define who we are so much by what we do professionally, having an opportunity to grow and advance is a critical element for keeping your top talent long-term. When people don't see a professional development opportunity or a chance for career advancement, they will seek opportunities outside of your organization. So, letting your new team members know from the beginning what growth opportunities they will have will help them to make permanent employment commitments to you and allow them to set goals for their future. Keeping our good people is critical to the overall development and well-being of our businesses, so neglecting this piece is a sure bet that you will constantly be in the hiring process—because your good people will leave when there is no room to grow!

This book's Resources section will provide you with a great sample for a professional development plan that works well.

Key #8: Create talent management tools to measure and reward your talent (and steps to help the "non-doers" leave).

A structured action plan worksheet for setting goals is a very simple way to allow your team members to hold themselves accountable. It also is an easy way for you to measure whether your people are doing what they said they were going to do!

Here's the deal: When someone is hired to do a specific job, he needs to honor his commitment to do his job. If you've set a solid onboarding process in place, provided a 30-, 60-, and 90-day review process to ensure everyone is on track for succeeding, and you have action plans in place for executing results, it's up to the employee to step into his role and take action. If he needs help, there should be support in place to help him. If he needs training, your training program should be well under way. And if he is hired to sell stuff, well…he better be showing you results!

Nine times out of ten when I see an employee leave an organization, it's because the business had the right person in the wrong job. So, there is something to be said about making sure the employee has the talent needed to fulfill his responsibilities. And if everything lines up—the talent fits the job, onboarding and training is provided, the employee has the free will to do his job—but you aren't seeing results, something has to change. And usually, it means finding a different job for the employee. Sometimes, the employee needs to leave.

We are a rewards-driven society. And in business, you have to reward the doers—the people who commit to getting the job done and follow through by doing what they said they would do! Again, it's about accountability.

The flipside of this proverbial coin is that when you don't hold your employees accountable, you are sending an equally powerful and often destructive message to everyone else on the team. It simply isn't fair to let some people off the hook when they don't execute. In fact, it's a key reason employee morale drops in an organization; what's the point of having goals if no one is going to carry them out? If I happen to be the superstar on the team who always produces results, but I work alongside someone who consistently doesn't follow through on his commitments, and we are paid the same and treated the same, why should I stay?

Rewarding performance is what will keep your good people happy. And holding the non-doers accountable for not contributing sets the foundation for your organization's culture to be one of excellence.

Key #9: Pay your people well!

It goes without saying that you need to pay your people what they are worth. If you haven't done so in a while, do some research on what your competition is paying its employees. Are you in the top 5 percent? You should be.

If you want the best, attract the best talent and pay them well so they do not leave. Money isn't everything, but when it comes to job satisfaction, research has shown that our income, benefits packages, rewards systems, and other intrinsic benefits of a job affect our overall wellbeing and commitment to our career jobs.

I don't suggest to my clients that they dig deeper into their pockets or tap into their children's college funds to increase their payroll—I'm talking about great rewards for great accomplishments. Find strategic ways your business can create more income for your hard-working team members. If you have a sales organization, it's easy to create high earning opportunities so your salespeople can earn bonuses and commissions on everything they sell! The greatest salespeople I have met approach their jobs with limitless earning goals—they know they are the only ones who will hold themselves back from achieving their income goals when they don't sell!

For those in non-sales related positions, opportunities should still exist for company profit-sharing or other rewards tied to performance, such as increased vacation time, a retirement plan, or leadership opportunities for personal and professional development.

Either way, make sure your people are proud of their earning opportunities, they know they are honored and paid well for their contributions, and they have some say in directing their earning power. Providing your employees with these advantages will increase their ownership in their work, which affects your bottom line substantially. No one should be entitled to income—a job should be about earning your value.

Key #10: Celebrate your accomplishments

How often do you and your team celebrate your accomplishments? Once a month? Once a year? Once in awhile?

I challenge all of my clients with one important goal: To have fun at work! And to celebrate the good stuff every single opportunity possible. Why not?

Some days, work is a challenge. In service organizations, we know that when that phone rings, someone's got a problem—and "it ain't always fun!" The non-profit groups I work with understand this situation more than anyone. Our clients count on us to help them, and sometimes it takes an extra dose of service, passion, understanding, and selfless effort to make things right. Giving in this way—often without seeing immediate results for our efforts—can feel heavy and depleting at times. Acknowledging good work is a vital part of keeping our talented people fueled and energized.

Create opportunities to have fun at work! Take notice when someone does something right and shine the light on those achievements, no matter how small. A simple acknowledgment can go a long way when it comes to employee satisfaction and building strong team morale. And it's so easy to do.

Many of my clients create fun sales contests in their offices; they hold teambuilding events or recognition programs; they go out for birthdays and holidays together, take time during the week to meet over lunch somewhere other than the office, or simply share life events with parties. It doesn't take a lot of time or money to have fun at work, but it does take intention and consistency.

Create a "Fun Committee" and assign someone on your team to drive the fun with you! You can gain greatly from your efforts, and improve morale instantly with a little dose of joy. (And YOU just might have more fun, too!)

To sum up the importance of inspiring your team through celebration, I think the famous management guru, Jack Welch, says it best:

> "Celebrating creates an atmosphere of recognition and positive energy. Imagine a team winning the World Series without champagne spraying everywhere. And yet companies win all the time

and let it go without so much as a high five. Work is too much a part of life not to recognize moments of achievement. Make a big deal out of them. If you don't, no one will."

FINAL THOUGHTS

Recruiting, training, and retaining talent is not easy, but it doesn't have to be hard. Know what your business needs, honor those needs, and make sure there is a perfect "fit" for all positions. Anything is possible when you have the right person in the right job. And getting that match right makes leadership gratifying.

CHAPTER EIGHT

ENSURING YOU HAVE THE RIGHT PEOPLE IN THE RIGHT JOBS: A SYSTEMS APPROACH

The working world would be a happier place if more of us aspired to roles that were just right—if we valued job fit and performance at every level and stopped overemphasizing the very top.

~ Nancy Lublin

I consistently see leaders holding themselves back by doing what they "think" they are supposed to do rather than crafting roles and responsibilities around the team's talent.

There is no one right way to run a business. There is no one way to lead an organization. Don't get me wrong; great leaders need to have certain competencies and abilities to take an organization to the next level. But I want to challenge you to take off the hats you wear, let go of traditional ways of getting things done, and tap into your own resource: your innate talent and your strengths. Set your strategic course from that place.

The best leaders I have researched have one consistent strategy in building a high-performance team: They have surrounded themselves with people who have skills and abilities that complement theirs, and who have talents they do not have.

If you truly intend to lead your team, and attaining team synergy is important to you, assessing your own talent, roles, and responsibilities has to come first. Once you assess and determine your strengths and weaknesses, you have a foundation upon which to build.

As a business owner, you might discover that you are the only true constant that will ever be tied to your business. Your team members will come and they may go, but as long as you are running this business, you will be the common denominator that will tie your team members, your clients, and your business partners to your business.

In the spirit of honoring your business, it all starts with you. If your job's roles and responsibilities do not line up with your innate talent and strengths, how do you expect to build a team of people who will run your business and increase results with you? It all starts with you.

In this process, I ask that you let go of traditional ways of getting things done. When it comes to the team members' roles and responsibilities, I don't care that you are the business owner. If you are excellent at multitasking and you love greeting people and directing traffic as they walk in or call into the office, then take over the front office desk a few times a week and have fun doing it! As long as you have other people fulfilling all of your business' needs, who cares who does what? The point is, figure out what you are good at and identify those things you love to do at work and do them! Do them as often as you possibly can. Not only will you enjoy your work more, but you will naturally begin to model this process of everyone stepping into his or her unique contribution to the team.

Just because you are the strategic leader, the "boss," the "CEO," doesn't mean you have to do it like the other guy down the street. As long as you don't abandon the responsibility of Leadership, you have the amazing privilege of crafting the job of your dreams. And when your entire team approaches the teambuilding process in this way, work becomes easy, gratifying, fun.

My second career job out of college was with a very talented and successful State Farm agent in Austin, Texas. By anyone's standards, this business owner, Nancy, is highly successful and adored by her peers. She is a driven business woman and has a great deal of pride in her business.

Over the years, Nancy has seen her business grow, with great profit. Her team is probably the highest paid team among her peers. Her philosophy is to pay them well, treat them with respect, get out of their way so they can do the job they've been hired to do, and honor the needs of her clients by having top-notch customer service. As Nancy prepares to celebrate 30 years in her business, she's doing an amazing job.

As her clientele grew, Nancy's team grew. And it has grown so much that she physically ran out of office space! She uses her kitchen for a pseudo-administrative office and she uses her conference room to run appointments.

Nancy has found, over the years, that she does her best work in the field—meeting her higher-end clients at their offices or in their homes. Work and personal responsibilities take her out of town frequently, so she is not physically in her main office some weeks. As a result, what made sense a few years ago was for Nancy to give her main office to her lead sales professional, who is also the office manager. Nancy's role is still that of CEO and Leader of her business; she communicates with the team daily, she has a rigid schedule of field appointments and travel commitments, and she runs a tight ship.

Nancy's role is a bit against the traditional role of running a State Farm Insurance Agency—but it is working beautifully! Her team members know what they are good at, they are clear about their roles and responsibilities, and they do their job well.

Nancy says the key to success when it comes to building a high performance team is having team members who have a positive, "can-do" attitude that take ownership of the business and have pride in the team's accomplishments. Many aspiring agents spend time in Nancy's office learning about the business and being mentored by her and her team as they prepare to launch their own businesses, and her less-than-traditional way of running her business operation is a perfect example of doing things differently while honoring the business' needs.

EIGHT STEPS TO ASSESS: DO YOU HAVE THE RIGHT PERSON IN THE RIGHT JOB?

Here is a simple eight-step formula to keep you on track until the day you close the doors to your shop.

1. Assess Your Team Talent.

Whether using assessment tools or not (we'll talk about assessment tools and how they help in the next chapter), I have found two powerful questions to help me get to the core of whether or not someone is in the right job.

First: What are you good at and what you do like to do (at work)?

Most people can answer that question without hesitation, listing things they innately know they are good at and love to do.

<u>Second</u>: Assess for yourself what the difference is between "a good working day" and "a bad (or unproductive) working day"?

Here is a simple activity that will help you identify these things:

<u>Activity</u>: Think about a time in your recent past where the day flew by. Work was easy, it was fun, and as you neared the end of the work day, you couldn't believe it was almost time to go home! An added bonus, you might have realized, is that you had all this energy—even though you were busy, you still had energy to go home and take on the tasks of the evening!

What happened that day? Describe the day in the space below:

_____

_____

_____

_____

Now I want you to think about the most recent day you had where you felt exhausted and depleted during the day: you looked at the clock several times, you couldn't believe how the day was dragging on, and you still had a list of tasks to complete! Closing time couldn't come soon enough, and all you wanted to do was get home and collapse—no time or energy for anything or anyone else.

What happened that day? Describe the day in the space below:

_____

_____

_____

_____

Chances are that in the first scenario you experienced a day where you were in your "flow"—you had the freedom to do things your way, you were doing tasks that were fun and easy for you, and productivity came naturally.

In the second scenario, I predict you were working against your grain… perhaps all day long!

As you evaluate the tasks of those days, you will quickly discover the aspects of your work for which you are naturally suited, and those where you get "stuck." The goal here is to start paying attention to what work creates energy for you, the fun stuff, and where you are working against your grain.

You may not have the luxury never to do those things for which you are not suited—that you either don't like or simply aren't good at— but when people understand why they are feeling depleted by working against their grain, somehow they are able to tolerate that pain with a little more patience.

Looking at the list of things you are good at, those things you like to do, how often do you get to incorporate those things into your work? How can you bring more of those activities into your day-to-day work functions? What would it take to make that happen?

And as you look at the list of things where you know you get "stuck," where you expend mental energy that holds you back from reaching high levels of productivity, how able are you to delegate those tasks to someone who is better suited to do them with ease? Is there a way to reduce the strain and stress associated with working against your grain? How can you make change now to increase your productivity?

I do this activity with my clients and their team members all the time. I emphasize that there are no promises here, but if we could barter and renegotiate the terms of our day-to-day tasks, what would that look like? How could we increase efficiencies?

Many times, my clients will discover through this process with their teams that they really do need more help. After the bartering process of roles and responsibilities for everyone on the team, it's always interesting and fun for me to see a team getting together to create a new job description for a potential new hire consisting of the list of tasks no one on the team is good at or likes to do! And hey, what's the big deal— there's almost always someone out there suited for the job when the others aren't. Here is where team alignment strengthens and trust deepens. And the "boss" doesn't need to figure it out alone.

2. Fine-Tune Job Descriptions Based on the Business' Needs.

Once a team has spent some time assessing talent, I like to work one-on-one with the team member to fine tune the person's job description. There are all kinds of templates out there to help create a basic job description for everyone on your team, but the key is to get the team members involved in this process.

If your team members already have job descriptions, make sure they pull them out regularly and review them with you, making sure their talents match their roles and responsibilities. Nothing is more powerful than giving your team members a voice in the creation of their jobs.

I have a client in New York who has recently revamped his entire business; in the process, everyone rewrote his or her own job description. Through one-on-one coaching sessions with each employee, the team members have drafted their new roles and responsibilities and presented them to the business owner. It has been a transformational process of renewed commitment and buy-in from all of the team members. They are excited about stepping into new roles and responsibilities, they are happy to have let go of the burden of some tasks that were weighing them down, and they are stepping up in a whole new way.

The gift in the process, to my client, is that he is not the only one driving this new feeling of commitment. He is coaching his team members and helping them to co-create their jobs. Employee satisfaction and increased performance are at an all-time high!

3. Rebalance: Who on the Team Best Fits the Job? Do You Need to Recruit New Talent?

The process of rebalancing is simple when you can answer these two questions:

1. What does the business need from the team?

2. Who is best suited for these tasks?

Before you go about the business of hiring new people or growing your team, do yourself a favor and spend some time seeing whether you have solutions by making some changes. Many times, when an employee leaves, we find out that we had the right person in the wrong job. Rebalancing is simply a matter of doing a check-up on your team talent and reassessing "fit." You should expect to do these reassessments at least once a year as a part of your strategic business planning.

Having the right people in the right jobs will keep the system balanced, and a happy team makes a happy business.

4. Hire Talent if a Gap Exists in Business Needs.

If you discover you have gaps in talent and the business requires that you hire someone new to fulfill that need, then enroll your team to co-create a job description for a potential new team member and start recruiting!

A thorough evaluation of your team talent might also dictate that you replace someone. Again, it all comes back to honoring the business' needs.

5. Collaborate with Team Members to Create Action Plans to Drive Alignment of Business Goals.

Once your team members have clear job descriptions and they know what is expected of them, help them to create their own Action Plans to achieve results.

Keep it simple. Ask each team member to identify three primary goals he or she wants to focus on for a stated amount of time (three months, six months, one year, etc.)

More than three will be too much. Three goals is perfect.

The **Goal Planning Worksheet** in the Resources section of this book is a simple worksheet that will allow your team members to set goals while acknowledging their unique strengths and skills to achieve results.

Bottom line: Your job is not to *tell* your team members what their goals are. Your job is to have them present to you what their goals are and the steps they wish to take to achieve them. Your objective is to keep them on task, make sure they are in alignment with company goals, coach and mentor them, and ask them regularly, "How can I help you achieve your goals?" Knowing what the team members need from you will help you to take them where they need to go. And when you give the ownership and accountability to the team, it frees you up to coach, mentor, and lead with intention.

Your team members are creative, resourceful, and whole. They need you to coach them, support them, provide them with needed direction, and give them feedback when they need it. As long as they stay on course and reach their target, you win.

6. Implement Accountability Measurement Tools.

Once your team has job descriptions in place, action plans for achieving results, and action plans to achieve them, it's vital that you check in with your team on a regular basis to see how they are doing. I recommend you check in at least monthly on a one-on-one basis to make sure they are being accountable for those results and you can measure whether the results are being achieved.

You can implement such measurement and follow-up on it in many ways, but I recommend you keep it simple. These performance reviews should be designed to get straight to the point so you can find out where the employee is having success and where he or she is feeling "stuck." Schedule a firm start and end time, stay focused on the goals and how they are being accomplished, and don't get caught up in conversation or other office issues that don't support this very important conference.

Here are the only questions I recommend you ask in this meeting:

- How are things going in your job? What's working well for you?

- Where are you feeling stuck? How can I help you to do your job better?

In these meetings, you want feedback. From the employee's point of view, how is he or she doing? And what does the employee need from you to do it better?

This meeting is also a perfect opportunity for providing feedback about what you are noticing. If someone is performing below expectations, you generally don't need to tell the person about it—he already knows where he is falling short! But you can work together to explore what's holding him back and create a plan for providing him with support to make a change.

Document your conversations. You will make the annual performance reviews easier and no one will ever be surprised about achieving results or falling short of commitments.

If at a second or third meeting, a conversation tends to repeat itself regarding someone's lack of performance, it's much easier to discuss making changes or helping the employee to find another job. It should never be a surprise when someone is let go. Failure to follow through on commitments, even when ongoing coaching and support is being provided, is all that is necessary to make the end of the relationship final.

7. Create Action Plans for Change.

Sometimes execution doesn't happen because of unrealistic expectations. It's important to evaluate whether this is the case when measuring results. When needed, adjust the action plan to compensate for unrealistic goals or altered goals. The beauty of putting something in a Word document is that you can go in and "tweak" it when you need to!

Change is the one certainty in business. Company initiatives and sudden changes in the business' needs can create a need for changing the course or direction. Ask any sailor who has taken off for a long sail—you constantly have to check the weather and the water currents, be alert to other vessels at sea, and change with the wind. Leading a team is no different, so staying fluid and flexible as you move forward will add a dimension of adventure and energy when you need it, rather than feel like chaos when change happens.

8. Repeat

Just a reminder that you will go through this process on a regular basis to achieve results. Leading your team through this process will ensure that you have the right team members in place at all times, making changes when you need to, anticipating what's around the corner.

The Resources section at the back of the book provides a sample of a simple performance review worksheet that you can use with your team development. These tools have been effective for my clients and you can refer back to them time and again.

CHAPTER NINE

TALENT-BASED ASSESSMENT TOOLS AND HOW THEY HELP

People often remark that I'm pretty lucky. Luck is only important in so far as getting the chance to sell yourself at the right moment. After that, you've got to have talent and know how to use it.

~ Frank Sinatra

Sometimes the act of figuring out what you're good at and what you like to do isn't an easy task. And learning to articulate what we know is true about ourselves is even more challenging!

In my quest to learn about talent, strengths, personalities, and cognitive abilities, and how they help to create a good "fit" for a job, I have discovered something very important: We can all get from "point A" to "point B," but the path we each take to get there is often very different.

I have seen some great leaders exhaust themselves trying to figure out why their people don't do it their way! The danger in measuring someone's performance based on doing it *your* way, instead of *their* way, is that you might be asking someone to perform a task that is completely against his or her grain! But the mistake we often make in leadership is summing up someone's actions based on our self-induced expectations of "how" he or she approaches things.

Our personalities, our strengths, our cognitive abilities, our innate talent—all of these things define who we are. Sadly, many people never take the time to self-assess these traits, so they stumble from one job to the next, trying to do it someone else's way, hoping that one day they will get it right.

In my work at the Gallup Institute, I realized something very powerful about how we look at strengths and weaknesses in our society, and it's no wonder we are at a crossroads when we are trying to be something we are not.

As children, we learn, at a very young age, what we're good at, and what we're not good at. Let's take Billy, a fourth grade student, for example.

Billy's teacher calls his parents and invites them in for a parent-teacher conference. During the meeting with the teacher, Billy's parents get a copy of Billy's report card. Billy got an A in science, a B in physical education, a C in language arts, and a D in math. All of his other classes were pass/fail, and Billy passed in those classes.

Guess how the conversation went down when the parents came home to review the meeting with Billy? I'm sure you can play this out, but let me illustrate my point:

Parents: Billy, you got a D in math! How did that happen?

Billy: I don't know. I hate math. It's dumb. I don't even know why I need to learn that stuff; it doesn't make sense.

Parents: Well, you need to try harder. We will have to spend more time working on your math with you so you can improve your grade. We'll get started today.

Billy rolls his eyes and runs off to play.

What about the A in science? Science is challenging for a lot of kids, but Billy seems to have a natural interest in science—it's easy and fun for him! If he could spend all day on science projects, he would LOVE school!

Rather than shining the light on the things where we excel, where we have natural success, with ease and joy, we are so conditioned to put emphasis on our deficiencies that we never get around to celebrating the good stuff!

The reality, as we know it, is that Billy needs to get passing grades to get through school so he can compete later on if going to college is his goal. We need to help making the learning process easier for Billy so he can make it through the system and manage those areas where he is falling short. Perhaps a tutor could help him make math a little less intimidating and more fun. But, frankly, Billy might never be excellent at math. And if you ask me, I say that's okay.

Billy, at a young age, is showing great interest in science. He loves participating in the science fair at school. He's naturally curious about the evolution of things and the cause and effect of how things work. What if we naturally celebrated Billy getting an A in science, and rather than spending a lot of extra time trying to get over his deficiency in math (by learning to manage it and simply getting up to "par"), we put extra emphasis on opportunities for him to excel in science—Billy could become a science expert!

We spend so much time trying to improve ourselves in the areas we learn we are not good at that we waste precious time and resources we could have spent on excelling in the things we already are great at! When we spend more time getting better at the things we already are good at, we become excellent! We break records; we set new standards for success. Focusing on what they are good at is what sets the superstars apart from all the others.

The same principle can be applied at work. If you look carefully and use some of the tools available to you to assess talent and strengths, you will find unique abilities in those you lead.

I would not proclaim that assessment tools are the answer to solving all of our people issues when it comes to creating a high-performance team. But the insight and learning you can acquire by incorporating assessment tools into your team development is invaluable. It allows for a third entity virtually to step into the room and shine the light on some truth about your team that you might not otherwise have realized. It makes the process of putting the right people in the right jobs a lot easier, and it provides support when you are feeling "stuck" with someone's performance.

I learned the hard way that the key to success in building a high-performance team is having the right people in the right job.

In the early years of my first business, I had a team of three. One of my team members had a long history working in my business. When the previous business owner retired and I took over as the new owner, she stayed on board with me. I hired two additional team members, and they were good employees.

The "inherited" employee gave me a run for my money. She just wouldn't perform the tasks I needed her to perform. She was hesitant to pick up the phone and make marketing calls, she never hit her production goals, and I was beginning to think she just didn't like me!

I spent many restless nights tossing and turning while I tried to figure out how I could get this employee to do what I needed her to do. And one night, I got a brilliant idea! So I called one of my friends to see what she thought.

Me: I know what I need to do to get my employee to sell more! I need to increase her bonus program! You know, I don't know why I didn't realize this sooner....If I want her to sell, I need to pay her more money!

Friend: Sounds like a good idea. But is she motivated by money?

Well, that was a silly question. I mean, who ISN'T motivated by money, right?

Wrong.

I ran to the office that morning, called an important meeting with my employee, and announced the beautifully enhanced, increased bonus program. In all its glory, I showed her how it would work, and with just a little extra effort, I knew she could make more money.

Employee: That's nice. Okay.

And then, she silently left my office.

I felt a little let down that she wasn't more excited about my proposal, but I thought if I just gave it a few weeks, she would soon see how much money was on the table for her to change her ways and she'd just do it!

Guess what? She wasn't motivated by money. She was motivated by more time off to go camping with her husband. She liked taking care of my clients and making sure they didn't go to our competitor, but making outbound calls to new potential clients was 100 percent against her grain and she had no desire to learn the process.

Was she in the wrong job? Of course she was! And some time after she left and went to work somewhere else, I realized she was not a good "fit" for my job. She was a good fit for another position in that office, but I didn't know then what I know now, so I lost some talent.

I have seen my clients increase bonus programs, rewrite benefits programs, give more time off, and bang their heads against a wall trying to get their team members to do something they will not do.

Don't get me wrong; we can all **do** things we don't like to do. But the staying power behind doing something against your grain will not last long.

Dozens of assessment tools are out there, and I encourage you to research those that apply to your needs. What's important to remember is that these tools are just additional sources of information to help you balance your team. Hire an expert who can help you to interpret the results and use the tools to help develop your people. If you do it right, assessment tools can be a valuable addition to your organization's success.

The biggest problem I see when it comes to assessment tools of any kind is the misuse of them. Companies waste thousands of dollars ordering tests, tools, and online questionnaires to help them understand their team members better. The information is often very interesting and useful, but the key is to make sure you are applying the information in a useful way. Only a licensed consultant who specializes in the tool's application can help you with the information's integration into your business.

I invite you to do your own research on assessment tools and find out what others in your industry are using for success. Then, hire someone to partner with you to interpret the results properly and help you to integrate the information into your teambuilding initiatives. It's a wonderful investment for your business when you do it right, and a great way to provide personal and professional development to your team members—something that has great value to employees today, especially when bonuses are down and raises aren't being granted.

Feel free to contact my team personally if you have specific questions about assessment tools. We will do our best to lend support and refer you to others who can help.

CHAPTER TEN

ACCOUNTABILITY FOR ACTION: LINKING REWARDS TO PERFORMANCE

If your actions inspire others to dream more, learn more, do more and become more, you are a leader.

~ John Quincy Adams

A key element in producing specific results is rewarding those who do the work! When rewards and respect are based on performance and it's clear to everyone that the act of getting it done is the goal, you begin to create a culture of execution.

I see a trend with my clients that, at first glance, is a notable and endearing quality: They are nice. "Nice" in a way that promotes affiliation and kindness, as a means to an end. But I have learned that being "nice" also can be very useless as a stand-alone quality in leadership. Some of my clients are also "nice" in a way that holds them back: Giving their people too many opportunities to *not* do the job they were hired to do.

Since when did showing up for work entitle everyone to rewards!? For goodness sake. Showing up for work doesn't entitle anyone to anything but compensation for doing exactly what they've been hired to do! And if they want to make *more* money they need to **do more**! Please shake your head and tell me you are with me on this one.

It's what sets the high performers apart from the rest. There are some team members who need to maintain our business—keep it running smoothly and make sure our valued customers don't leave us. But for those employees who want to earn more, who are motivated by rewards (which are packaged in many forms), they want an opportunity to do more! They want to perform and be rewarded for their efforts.

By linking rewards to team members' performance, you do three vital things:

1. You create a greater sense of responsibility and more ownership of the job to the employee.

2. You stimulate the employee to work harder than he or she might otherwise do.

3. You give the employee some control over his or her income.

Let's look at each of these vital points in detail:

1. Creating Responsibility

Having ownership in your work is a sure way to increase "buy in" and responsibility. It's like having some "skin in the game"—something to lose when you don't get it right.

One of biggest mistakes I see leaders make is thinking they have to do it all themselves. If you are privileged to lead a team, give yourself permission to let your team help you to get where you need to go!

I facilitate a lot of planning retreats for teams. One of the most important activities I do in designing a planning meeting for a team is gaining clarity on where the team is having success and where the team is
stuck—from *everyone's* point of view (not just the boss').

The feedback I get during a team assessment helps to define the work
that needs to be done. And when each participant shows up around my
table, we begin with blank sheets of paper that allow for everyone to
participate in the problem-solving process.

Nothing is more empowering for a team member than helping to craft
his or her own roles and responsibilities. When an individual is allowed
to take ownership over driving results, affecting change, and helping to
co-create the action steps needed to get the job done, he will resist the
temptation to compromise on his commitments.

Additionally, our team members will come up with ideas and solutions
we might never think of individually! Collaborating on action plans
and allowing everyone to step-up and contribute will spike buy-in and
action more than any amount of money or other incentive I have seen.
We all have a voice. And we each want our voice to be heard. Let your
team members own their work and proclaim what is theirs to achieve.
It will make your work as the leader easier and it will be more gratifying
for everyone.

2. Stimulating Hard Work

When someone has a sense of purpose in her work, when she values
excellence in work, she is less likely to compromise her contribution.
And motivated team members are more likely to work harder and more
effectively.

What I have witnessed is that the most motivated team members are those who have had the opportunity to get involved in the design of their incentive programs.

I have a client who regularly reviews his incentive programs. What I have found useful about this process is that he involves the entire team in the business planning process, allowing his team members to take ownership over certain aspects of the business plan for driving results. Ownership at this level is powerful. It gives each of the employees a purpose and a sense of contribution that is linked to the overall business objectives. It's smart. And it's a strategic and easy way to get your team engaged and committed.

Once everyone knows what she is responsible for in terms of driving results, she can begin to put rewards to goals. Get your team members involved in this process!

Some team members find great value in things that don't involve income. Things like flex-time, extra vacation time, insurance or retirement benefits, awards or incentives that are tied to results, can create a great sense of pride for achieving goals. It is acknowledgement at its core—finding out what is most important to your employees, their values and personal goals—and linking rewards for their individual accomplishments.

Another important factor in carrying out results with excellence is a process for ongoing feedback and management of results. That is where performance reviews come into play.

A certain stigma exists when I use the term "performance review" with my clients. For many managers, performance reviews are a heavy task that can be full of negativity and shine the light on "what's wrong."

However, I find performance reviews to be fascinating! And I have come to realize that the problems come not so much from the performance review process itself so much as the tracking process and tools we use to do it.

Here's the deal: Performance reviews don't have to be long, laborious, negative meetings! Let your team member come to you and sit down to discuss where she is having success and where she is "stuck" so you can coach and mentor her. Do it frequently! Make sure goals are attainable and that the employee has the tools, training, and processes in place to achieve the goals.

Having accountability measures in place are necessary if you want to achieve results. But keep it simple. Let your team member drive it. All of these elements need to be in place if you are going to link rewards to performance with success:

- The right person in the right job

- A clear job description with defined roles and responsibilities, co-created with the employee

- A professional development plan that ensures the employee is getting the tools and training he or she needs to succeed

- Regular performance reviews to find out what's working and where the employee gets "stuck"

- Ongoing evaluation of goals and how the employee is doing in achieving them

- Frequent conversations about the rewards system to ensure it lines up with the employee's personal goals and values

#3. Giving Employees Control Over Their Income

Employees in sales positions need great incentives! Sometimes that means money, sometimes it's time off; sometimes it's an award system for gaining credentials or increased learning. The key element here is to design an opportunity for your team members to have control over what they earn—reward them!

One of my clients has a salary plus bonus program for his sales team. When the employee is on-boarded, this base plus bonus is available on day one. However, when the employee reaches a certain level of income, he has the choice to stay where he is or to transition to a commission-only program, which provides an even more lucrative income. This second option is ideal for someone who wants full control of his income earnings! It's brilliant.

Many ways exist to reward employees through income. And I always recommend having conversations about pay and income separate from performance reviews! (Or at least designing the income section of the conversation as a separate entity.)

Money motivates and it helps people to tie value to their work. And in my experience working with sales teams, nothing is more powerful than an unlimited income potential!

Your sales professionals need to know how to make money and top producers will constantly be looking for more efficient ways to get the job done.

An added tip: Help your front-line sales team to hire an administrative assistant so that more of their time can be spent in the sales process, and provide ongoing training to increase their productivity. It will make the entire process more successful and fun for everyone.

Some people just love to sell. They love the challenge of uncovering the needs of the client and creatively crafting solutions to fill those needs. And if it's an excellent product, it's a win-win for both the salesperson and the customer, right?

In my work as a sales recruiter, I am fascinated to find so many people (who are just like me) and have absolutely no problem being paid commission only. But here is where we lose the good candidates: When the product isn't excellent, when the salesperson doesn't believe in the product, and when there is a limit on how much the salesperson can make, it doesn't last. All of those elements have to be there in order for paid commission to work.

I helped one of my clients to hire a front-line sales producer recently. In one of the final interviews the candidate said to me, "Theresa, I'd really like to take this job. But I need to make at least $60,000 this year to accept the position just to pay my bills! How can I achieve this goal and possibly make more?"

I said, "Joe, ask the Agent to show you how you can do that. There's no limit on what you can earn if you aren't afraid to get in there, pick up the phone, and fill up your appointment book. Figure out how you can do it, and go for it."

Joe accepted the job. And it's 100 percent on him to produce the results. The work environment has systems and processes in place to allow him to do it if he is truly committed, and we expect great results. He has a minimum quota that he must meet just to keep his job, and beyond that, it's on him as to how much he wants to make.

Who has control of his or her income now? It's a partnership between employee and employer, and ultimately up to the employee to do whatever he or she can to achieve results.

Final thoughts on linking rewards to performance:

Having a sense of control and ownership in our work and knowing our performance directly impacts our rewards, monetarily and intrinsically, is a powerful way to establish a culture of accountability and excellence. However, it doesn't work for those who enjoy passively showing up for work and punching a clock. If you've got "clock-punchers" whom you wish to have crank it up a notch, you might consider reevaluating your performance measurement tools.

CHAPTER ELEVEN

CREATING A CULTURE OF EXCELLENCE FOR YOUR BUSINESS

Be Famous for Something!

~ Anonymous

If you want to be known for something, you better know what you are good at and then deliver. And if someone is going to refer business to you, that person has to know what you are good at!

If you are craving a great cheeseburger and some fries, you go to McDonalds, right? But if you want fried chicken served in a bucket to share, you go to KFC! Buy in bulk? Go to Costco. You want a good neighbor to be your friend and take care of your family's insurance needs—go see a State Farm Agent! You'd like old fashioned service with a smile for your hardware needs? Stop by your neighborhood Ace Hardware store.

You can see where I'm going with this, and I could go on all day about branding your business and being known for something. But what I'm really referring to is creating a culture for your business: A predictable, dependable, consistent experience that you are known for when a client does business with you and with your team.

When a client crosses the threshold of your business, what does he experience? And more importantly, is that experience the same experience that you intend for him to have? What about the next time he comes to your place of business? Is that experience consistent, predictable, the same experience as the first time he arrived? If you can answer "Yes!" to this question, without hesitation, you can skip this chapter. In fact, take your team out on the town and celebrate the fact that you have achieved what most businesses only dream of achieving one day—a culture of outstanding customer service resulting in exceptional results, consistently. For the rest of us, I'll dedicate this section to creating a culture of excellence by honoring the business and your clients' needs.

I spent a couple of years working for Hertz Car Rental Agency at the Missoula International Airport in college. I remember the owner telling me that our rental fees would always be competitive, but we were not the "cheapest." For someone going counter-to-counter to check prices, our price could always be beat, even if only by a few dollars. However, I learned that we had the best quality fleet of vehicles, exceptional service, and the best location for a rental counter at the airport. We prided ourselves upon being "#1."

To this day, Hertz positions itself as the #1 Car Rental Agency for corporations. It caters to the busy traveler's needs, and has more corporate contracts around the globe than any other Car Rental agency, but it also has prices that its competitors can always beat. So, why is Hertz still #1? Because it is known for having the first point of contact for passengers arriving at the car rental counters, it has consistent high ratings for the quality of its customer service, it is known for having a wide variety of high-quality vehicles in its fleet, and it offers VIP services that are second to none when it comes to the savvy business traveler. No one has been able to do it better from point A to point B, and Hertz remains "famous" for the product and experience its customers will have no matter where they are traveling, throughout the world.

Of course, the occasional misnomer occurs where the customer service is less than fabulous and customer complaints appear, but that is rare. Hertz has done an outstanding job over the years of creating a customer experience that is second to none, and its team works hard to compete for that title.

When is the last time you took an audit on your customers' experiences with your business? If it's been a while, here's a chance for you to take inventory and find out whether the experiences your clients are having are in alignment with your business goals. Following are five key points.

1. Know Your People and Your Business.

If executing exceptional service to your clients is important to you, you have to be in the trenches of your business' day-to-day realities. Leaders must *live* their businesses.

I've been fascinated by the TV show *Undercover Boss*, a reality show that has some of America's top executives going into their companies' trenches to get a taste of "real life" on the frontline. Why is this show so powerful that it gained so much attention in the media? I think it's the human element of building a business and making employees feel appreciated that resonates so much for the viewers every week.

People have always thought, "I wish my boss knew what I do. I want to make a difference, but nobody notices me." Or, "I have some ideas, but I don't feel like anyone cares." This show has highlighted some powerful stories about the people on the business' frontlines.

One of my favorite episodes featured the restaurant Hooters (a restaurant and bar known for its famous "wings," and whose first restaurant featured topless waitresses!) Profits for Hooters had been down in 2010, and leadership wanted to figure out how to increase business.

As the CEO went undercover and got into the trenches of the day-to-day business operation alongside some of the employees, he realized some critical realities: He had no clue how many people thought his company was demeaning toward women and that women (and families) didn't want to go into his place of business. (These days, the waitresses at Hooters restaurants aren't topless, but they still sport tight tank tops, leaving little to the imagination.)

He also discovered how poor leadership impacted business. One of his top-producing locations was managed by a womanizer who humiliated his employees and disgraced the company. How could someone end up in a management role with such poor leadership skills?

Like most companies, Hooters needed to acknowledge its people. After the Hooters' owner saw what his company was like on the frontline, he decided to make several changes. Now, as the company puts new systems and processes in place and leaders who deserve to hold those roles, it will increase workers' pride in their work, which in turn could help the restaurant chain to succeed in offering the public a more consistent experience. It will be interesting to see whether things change for Hooters…because, they DO have good wings.

The reality is that a business' human capital—its team and the players on it—is its greatest resource. Human capital is arguably the most valuable asset held by an organization today. This capital simultaneously represents the single greatest potential asset and the single greatest potential liability an organization will acquire as it goes about its business.

Ask yourself: How balanced is your team's scale?

- Are you investing in your people?

- Do they have clear job descriptions?

- Do they have a professional development plan to guide them?

- Is everyone committed and engaged?

2. Know Yourself.

Emotional fortitude: It's a vital part of being honest with yourself. Let's face it; it isn't always easy to take a look in the mirror and hold your gaze. But that reflection defines your true reality. And part of leading is having the courage to stand in your absolute truth, even when it's hard.

Here is where things tend to get emotional. I get emotional writing about my role in my business, because, for me, it's taken years to figure out what my real contribution is to my business and to my clients. I wish I could do it all and be it all. But frankly, I'm not good at everything. And, as the great innovator Michael Dell once said, "The key to success is in surrounding yourself with people who are better than you."

As I mentioned right off in Chapter 1, leadership is not for the faint of heart. Once we are clear on our role as a leader, it takes courage to step into it and strategy to design a path that others will follow.

Here are some questions to ask yourself about your role as a leader:

- What are my greatest assets?

- How do I best contribute to my organization?

- What do my clients count on from me as the leader of my team?

- What do my team members need from me so I can lead them successfully?

3. Know What Sets You Apart from Your Competitors.

If you've ever been to a Krispy Kreme donut shop, you know exactly what sets Krispy Kreme apart from its competition—an absolutely fun, tasty, and entertaining experience! As you step into the store, you immediately feel the excitement of a less than usual donut buying event: the floor to ceiling windows showcasing conveyor belts full of tasty donuts, bakers busily pacing the bakery floor, music playing, merchandise displayed, and at the end of the line, standing in anticipation as your mouth salivates with impatience, FREE DONUTS hot off the assembly line, glazed in frosting, melting in your mouth as your eyeballs take in the beauty of some of the most glorious donut delights you have ever seen!

Taking my two young boys to Krispy Kreme for the first time was like a mini-vacation to Disneyland. They were fascinated to watch the donuts as they were cooked in hot oil, then flipped perfectly as they approached the wall of tumbling frosting, and needless to say, my sons were thrilled with the free donuts waiting for them at the end of the line.

Already full from free donuts, I of course felt obligated to buy a dozen more, along with chocolate milk, gourmet fruit juice, and coffee, and to take a seat with the other patrons there for the donut party.

Krispy Kreme has created an experience like no one in the donut industry has ever come close to, and taking a box of Krispy Kreme donuts to any event is a royal treat. The company has created a culture that is its own, and it keeps people coming back for more.

THIS customer experience is exactly what I'm talking about when I ask my clients why I, as a customer, would pick their business over a competitor's!

If you have something to offer that no one else can, shout it out at the top of your lungs!

If you give all of your new clients a traveling coffee mug stashed with candy so they remember you every morning on their commute to work, isn't that a great thing? When I go to the grocery store holding your company mug in my hand and the clerk says, "Hey, that's a cool coffee mug!" I can say, "Yes, my State Farm Agent gave me this as a thank you when I bought my new home insurance. She does that for all of her clients!"

Maybe that sounds like a bit of a stretch, but it's a true story. My State Farm Agent DID give me a beautiful black travel mug lined with rhinestones and people comment on it ALL THE TIME! My insurance agent, Vickie Bergquist, does things like that. She provides gifts to her clients that represent her business, and she has become known for her generosity and caring nature as she provides her clients with useful gifts. She also sends me address labels during the holidays, which I use annually and appreciate greatly.

4. Make Sure Your Clients Know How to Refer People to You.

The key to your clients giving you unlimited referrals is to make it as easy as possible for them to give you referrals! And if they aren't clear about what it is you specialize in, how can they tell their friends about you?

Educating your clients about your products and services is a vital part of building your business. And asking a simple question like, "Who do you know that might also benefit from our services?" is a powerful and simple way to get some referrals!

If you know your clients have had an exceptional experience working with you and your team, ask them to help you spread the word. Tell them what you want, which is to grow your business with other clients just like them, and let them know what an honor it would be to gain their trust through referrals. If you've got something great to offer, help your clients to know how to market and refer you. Do it daily.

5. Make Sure Your Colleagues and Customers Fully Understand All of Your Products and Service Offerings.

The average professional has many people in his or her active business network, yet many of those contacts don't truly understand all of the professional's product or service offerings.

If you don't believe this is true, all you need to do is show a client or colleague a list of your products or services and watch for his typical response, "Wow! I never knew you did that, too!"

The important lesson in this piece is never to take for granted that your clients, or the team that you lead, understands the depths of your services and specialties. Make it easy for people to know how to utilize your services by shining the light brightly on your talent and your skills.

CHAPTER TWELVE

CULTURE AUDITS AND WHY THEY MATTER

Who knows what is good and what is bad?
~ Taoist parable

Planning and facilitating off-site planning retreats and teambuilding events is one of my favorite things to do as an Executive and Team-building Coach. Usually the team leader or HR director reaches out to me for help in designing a meaningful, off-site event that will stimulate change and create alignment for everyone on the team.

Because pulling an entire team out of the office for an entire day affects productivity and requires resources from the business, we need to make sure the day is impactful and effective. And if we get it right, we make powerful shifts with the team to improve results, strengthen team alliance, and regain commitment from everyone on the team.

Through this very strategic work, I have discovered that the only way to design an off-site event for a team or to create a team development program for results is to thoroughly assess the team's needs at every level. The most effective tool I have found to accomplish this process is something called a Team Culture Audit, which is simply the study and examination of an organization's cultural characteristics (such as its assumptions, norms, philosophies, and values) to determine whether those characteristics hinder or support the organization's vision and mission.

Here's what I think is important about this process: As team leader, your only perspective is your own—the lens you look through every day. Your own personal experiences and your limited feedback influence you, and without collective data from everyone on the team, it's hard to understand the true reality of the team's culture and state.

What you want to strive for when it comes to organizational assessment and change is awareness at a very high level, the "meta-view" of what is really true about your organization. And the only way to achieve that meta-view is through a process of deep democracy, where every voice is heard and every perspective is a part of the collective data needed to evaluate the true state of reality within a team or organization.

Deep Democracy™ is a coaching concept I learned through my work with the Coaches Training Institute, the oldest training organization in the industry that sets the standards for the coaching industry. Deep Democracy, a term developed by physicist Arny Mindell, is a methodology developed to foster a deeper level of dialogue and inclusivity.

Deep Democracy is a way of working with people that allows for all voices to be heard. As defined, "*Deep democracy* is typified by accepting the simultaneous importance of all voices and roles. *As long as there is a sense that one person or level is more important than another, deep democracy is not at hand.* In deep democracy, rank and no rank exist simultaneously."[1]

---

1 Taken from: http://www.aamindell.net/deep-democracy.htm

Deep Democracy's emphasis is on both the individual and collective processes—all are equally important for knowing what is true and understanding the totality of the process.

When working with a team, the only way to gain deep democracy and find out exactly what is "true" of the business' culture is to call everyone forward so every voice is heard. This process is a realization and acknowledgment that everyone is needed to represent reality. The tool that I have found works best is a confidential culture audit questionnaire.

The culture audit asks each team member, including the team leader, to respond to a series of confidential questions. The collective data provide a snapshot of what's working well within the organization, and where the team gets "stuck." It is a powerful process of discovery and often lends the team leader significant feedback about potential "hot spots" that may need immediate attention.

With this collective data, I am able to provide my best service in designing organizational development and systems work for great effectiveness.

When conducting a team culture audit, the questions should be simple. They should be sent online to each participant, and room for feedback should always be included so the employee can freely add comments, from his or her perspective.

In addition to basic facts, such as listing name (optional), number of years in the organization, etc., I have used the following core questions to conduct insightful team culture audits, which can be customized to fit your needs:

1. I have a clear job description and know what my job duties are?

Yes   No

Please explain:

_____

_____

_____

_____

2. I am provided with job training that allows me to do my job better and with more ease:

Never   Rarely   Sometimes   Almost Always   Always

Please explain:

_____

_____

_____

_____

3. I feel driven to make a difference in my organization:

Never   Rarely   Sometimes   Almost Always   Always

Please explain:

_____

_____

_____

_____

4. In your opinion, what inspires people to make a difference in the organization?

_____

_____

_____

_____

My organization recognizes and celebrates successes of team members:

Never   Rarely   Sometimes   Almost Always   Always

Please explain:

_____

_____

_____

_____

5. How could your team improve the way it recognizes the successes of individual team members?

_____

_____

_____

_____

6. We work together as a team:

Never   Rarely   Sometimes   Almost Always   Always

Please explain:

_____

_____

_____

_____

7. What do you believe are important characteristics of a good team?

_____

_____

_____

_____

8. My organization communicates effectively (written and verbal) and in a timely manner to its employees:

Never   Rarely   Sometimes   Almost Always   Always

Please explain:

_____

_____

_____

_____

9. I enjoy starting a new day:

Never   Rarely   Sometimes   Almost Always   Always

Please explain:

_____

_____

_____

_____

10. What makes a really good day for you?

_____

_____

_____

_____

11. Describe what makes your organization great and what could make it better?

_____

_____

_____

_____

12. What does your organization need to be focused on to be successful for the next year?

_____

_____

_____

_____

13. If you could implement any change within your organization, what would it be?

_____

_____

_____

_____

Feedback from these questions will help to shine the light on what is truly going on within the organization and help you to identify areas of team synergy as well as areas of strain or conflict among the team players. Often when I review the collective feedback from this process I can immediately help the team leader to understand why the team is "stuck," and collectively, we can begin putting a plan in place for team-building, heightened awareness, and solutions for creating a stronger team alliance.

Honoring the system as its own entity, and accepting that each of the parts (the people), make up the organization's whole will help you, as Leader, to understand more clearly your business opportunities and potential threats. And you don't have to do it alone. The gift in this process is that when you hold each of your team members up to being creative, resourceful, and whole (another concept adopted from the Coaches Training Institute), you don't have to figure it all out on your own. With this powerful feedback, you can begin to put your strategy in place for taking action—then, you'll be one step closer to intentional productivity.

CHAPTER THIRTEEN

WHAT GETS IN THE WAY OF GETTING THINGS DONE?

*We're all so often caught up in the **Whirlwind** of our day jobs that we don't get a chance to focus on the **Wildly Important Goals**.*
~ Stephen R. Covey

The concept of Covey's "whirlwind" is nothing new to business teams, but it sure is validating when you realize you aren't alone in getting caught up in these whirlwinds at work and in life.

What keeps most of us from changing course or executing a new strategy? The daily grind. Covey talks about the "whirlwind" of competing priorities and fire drills.

What I think we can all relate to the most is the frustration in knowing there is much to be done and so little time to do it! And when we are constantly being interrupted all day long and are taken off of our productivity course, it's emotionally and physically exhausting.

I'm not a maker of checklists, but sometimes I need one to keep myself "on track"—to keep me out of trouble. For those of you with the innate instinct to follow a plan, I understand your pain when you don't have the freedom to follow the items on your list! And for those of you who lead "busy" teams (I assume anyone reading this book would say that is the case for him or her), it's very easy to get pulled in many directions and never quite get back to that "to do" list.

Let me put this in simple terms: If you show up for work every day and begin by simply reacting to everything that is going on around you, how will you ever be able to take care of the business' needs?

Strategic business planning is easy. When you are driving, or running, or dreaming about the possibilities of your work and your business, you are always in a state of endless possibilities. Some of you might even take time to write your brilliant ideas on paper, or say them out loud to your loved ones or co-workers! It's exciting to allow yourself this creative time to think, to brainstorm, and to consider the "bigger picture" of what is possible with your work. The hard part is the *doing*. And when you are in a constant state of reaction to the business' day-to-day demands, it's easy to feel defeated and hopeless about getting ahead.

In this chapter, we are going to take some time to consider what gets in our way and holds us back from executing, from getting the job done with ease. At the chapter's end, you can list your own personal and professional "whirlwinds" that keep you stuck. Our task in this process is to begin simply noticing what some of the whirlwinds are—we don't have to "fix" anything yet—so we can become prepared when the rumble is starting to build.

A BUSINESS' NEEDS

Have you ever held an off-site planning conference with your team where you got your team members all fired up, believing that everyone was recommitted to their jobs, and had everyone feeling good about the future as they walked away with a new business plan in hand and renewed energy for the business?

…And three months later, you begin wondering what happened to all of the excitement that you had a few months ago as you witness your team not reaching its goals. Six months later, you wonder where those flipcharts from the meeting went. And nine months later, you pull your team together for a "talk" to ask why everyone isn't doing what he said he was going to do last fall at the planning meeting.…

Here's the deal: Your business needs a simple and straightforward business plan with a list of goals, measurable action plans to achieve those goals, and a reward system in place for achieving them.

Ask yourself these vital questions:

- What do my clients need from my business?

- What does my business need from me?

- What do I need from my team in order to achieve our goals?

What we have to do is break down these very simple and critical elements for getting it right. If we are not honoring both our clients and our business' needs, we have no lens to look through to make those important day-to-day decisions about what needs to be done. And if we are constantly in a state of reaction every day at work, how will we even know whether we are on track for getting anything done?

It's all about intention. If everyone on your team isn't aware of what the organization's goals are, what their individual roles and responsibilities are for getting things done, and no accountability measures are in place, you can't expect to achieve the results you want. If you do achieve them, it will be by complete accident. And is "by accident" any way to run a business? Probably not.

Make sure systems and processes are in place at every level to achieve results. If your team is spending time and energy on things that do not directly impact the results you have collectively created, they simply need to quit doing them. Or, you might have to let your non-doers move on to another job or another career where they can achieve results. You've got a business to run—there's just "no room at the inn" for the non-doers. I'm sorry, but there's just no way I can candy-coat that one: Your people need to do what they've been hired to do.

OUR PEOPLE—OUR TEAM

Oh, our people. They make us, they break us—they make us laugh and they make us cry. When we get it right, it's like the best drug anyone ever invented—what joy! What excitement when you have a team that performs with excellence—people who like their work and are good at what they do! I can't think of anything more gratifying for a team leader.

But when we have the right people in the wrong jobs, or simply the wrong people on our team, it's like being at the bottom of a deep dark well with nothing but despair to guide us. It's a lonely and frustrating thing to deal with when you have a team that doesn't perform—it's the thing that keeps team leaders and business owners up at night. It sucks the energy out of us and affects many aspect of our lives – at work and at home.

Maybe I'm being a little dramatic, but if you've ever managed a team of any kind or run a business that required employees, you know what a challenge it is to recruit and retain excellent talent. It's the #1 issue that employers face and the biggest ingredient to high achieving business teams. You can't bluff this one.

I recently read a fascinating article at Salary.com that summarized a study on wasting time at work. The study surveyed 2,500 people in all lines of work, almost evenly split between men and women and 90 percent as full-time employees. What the research showed is that a record number of people waste time at work. Of course, I was curious to find out why. After all, if we have so much to do that gets in our way of getting things done, who's got time to waste, right? Here are some of the results from the study:[1]

> Sixty-four percent of respondents report wasting one hour or less each day, 22% waste approximately 2 hours daily, and 14% waste 3 or more hours each workday....This year, 73% of the survey participants indicated that they spend part of their day on activities that are not work-related, a 10% increase over last year's number.

The study revealed that the top time wasting activities were, in this order: Internet use, socializing with co-workers, conducting personal business, personal phone calls, and taking long lunches and breaks. In addition, the study found that:

> Twenty-two percent of respondents admit to wasting up to two hours per day, down slightly from 24 percent in 2007. Interestingly, data indicates that individuals with a Bachelor's degree or higher tend to waste slightly more time during the workday. This is likely

---

1 You can view the full article at: http://www.salary.com/Articles/ArticleDetail. asp?part=par1083

due to the fact that these individuals hold higher-level positions within their organizations and are not under close supervision....

Employees 50 and over waste the least amount of time, with 49% reporting they waste a half hour or less each day. Only 13% waste between 30 minutes and an hour. Thirteen percent waste approximately 2 hours per day and only 5% report wasting 3 or more hours. They also tend to spend more time conducting personal business than their younger counterparts.

The study went on to ask people why they wasted time. Their most popular reasons, in this order, were: being unsatisfied with their type of work, feeling underpaid, lack of deadlines or incentives, work hours that were too long, and distractions from fellow employees, friends, and relatives.

None of these findings surprised me. When you aren't in a job that fits your talent, and your talent isn't being utilized, it's easy to disengage! This study shows us the propensity for wasting time when you are in a job that you either don't like or simply are not good at.

And when there aren't reward systems in place for achieving results (aka: money, personal incentives), how committed do we really expect our people to be?

The main points I took away from this very interesting and alarming survey are:

- If we don't have the right people in the "boat," we aren't going to get very far in navigating our course.

- If everyone in the "boat" isn't rowing in the same direction, we will likely get "stuck" and get nowhere very fast.

- If our team members are not motivated and we fail to provide motivation so they share our vision, we are not going to move forward.

- If our talented team members don't have the right training, processes, and systems in place to allow them to succeed with intention every day, we are expending unnecessary resources.

Our people are our greatest resource; there is no room for negotiating this fact.

NOT HONORING OURSELVES

As if it's not enough that our business and the people we lead and manage every day demand so much from us to ensure we stay on track, I'd like to present to you what I believe is the #1 thing that gets in the way of getting things done: You.

As you've heard me say before in this book, and as I have said in countless coaching sessions and workshops with my clients, sometimes you simply have to get out of your own way in order to achieve results.

What do I mean by "Get out of your own way"? Let me try to explain by telling you a story. A personal story about a "Gremlin" of mine called Pity Perfect.

I have Gremlins. We all do. But I seem to have a few that have been with me for many, many years. Bestselling author Rick Carson has written several books about taming gremlins, including *Taming Your Gremlin: A Surprisingly Simple Method for Getting Out of Your Own Way.* Carson also runs a "Gremlin-Taming Institute," and he has been educating us for years about what he has coined as the "Gremlin."

In *Taming Your Gremlin*, Carson explains:

> For many of us, the voice of the Gremlin is that voice that tells you whatever you're doing isn't good enough. The Gremlin tells you that no matter how much you've improved your life, you still have a long way to go.
>
> The Gremlin speaks in "shoulds" and "coulds" and holds you back. They prevent us from reaching goals or reaching our potential. And when we listen to the Gremlin, we're kind of stuck. There's absolutely no way you can live the life you want to live if you let these voices run your life.

Through my work with my executive coach, Jeaneen, and from years of studying Carson's work, I have learned to personify and give a name to my most annoying "Gremlin"—Pity Perfect.

Pity Perfect is a terrible pest of mine. She shows up with vigor and a very loud voice every time I attempt to take on a new challenge or something I've never done before! She says things like, "Who are you to think you can take on that new project? You've never done something like that before—you aren't good enough to do that, so why bother? If it's not perfect, why do it at all?"

Thanks to great coaching and a bit of Carson's humor in the "Gremlin-taming" process, I have learned simply to "notice" when Pity Perfect shows up. Carson says these Gremlin voices usually show up when we're faced with change, doing something new, or starting something new: Taking on new challenges!

Now, as a student of Gremlin Taming, I have learned that I might never completely get rid of my Gremlin. However, I can learn to tame it (or at least turn down the volume of its voice). Once, when I had the opportunity to talk to Rick Carson, he described Gremlin-taming to me by saying, "It's not about the cartoon character or the angel sitting on one shoulder and the Gremlin on the other. It's about freeing yourself from your entire dialogue."

I suggest you read Carson's books on Gremlin-taming if you want to learn more—they are a fun and brilliant read. I feel he has a powerful message for all of us: You are the only one who will get in the way of getting things done.

Getting out of your own way is about honoring yourself and what you know is true. What are you good at? What do you love to do? What tasks, when under pressure and when everything falls on you, do you find exhilarating and fun? How often do you dedicate time each day to doing those things?

In the space below, I want you to write at least three things that you are good at and love to do at work.

1._____

2._____

3._____

And now, in the following space, I want you to reflect on when you last did these things and how often you get to do them every day.

_____
_____
_____
_____

If it's been a while since you, as leader or business owner, have updated your job description, now is the time to do it.

Just like your team, when you have the freedom to do what you are good at, you will find success with ease and results driven by intention.

It's time to have a talk with yourself and to get clear on your roles and responsibilities as leader of your team so you can take your team where you need to go.

Your clients are counting on you. And so is your business.

CHAPTER FOURTEEN

WHAT DOES THE BUSINESS NEED?

COMPETE WITH CLASS and HONOR THE GAME
* *Respect your coaches, teammates, opponents, officials, and the fans.*
* *Compete with heart, honor, and hustle.*
* *Honor the traditions of the game and respect the ancestors of the sport.*
* *Have fun, be passionate, and adhere to the spirit of the game both on and off the field.*

~ U.S. Lacrosse Code of Conduct

My oldest son has been playing lacrosse for about five years. He loves the sport. He loves the sport's discipline. It's a big commitment for our entire family for him to be able to play and compete. And it's incredibly fun to watch!

What has impressed me the most about this sport is the level of integrity upheld by the coaches and athletes and the motto the boys regularly chant, "Honor the Game." There is nothing about personal gain in this sport compared to many other sports; it's about the contribution each player is required to make toward the good of the team and of the game. What an amazing life lesson for these young men who day-after-day stand in the rain, the sleet, the snow (yes, I live in Seattle and our springs can be tough!) and strive for excellence. It is so inspiring.

What resonates so much for me in this message is the need for all of us, as true leaders, to honor our "sport"—our businesses! Are we making intentional, wise, and courageous decisions on a daily basis to do what's best for our business?

My clients can count on me to ask them this question over and over during our coaching relationship: "What does the business need?" From you? From your team? When you are faced with decisions, are you honoring the business' needs in the choices you make?

One of my clients called the other day, very frustrated with an employee's lack of productivity. I'll call my client "Sue" to protect her confidentiality. Sue hired an employee about a year ago; Sue gave the employee time to adjust to her new work environment, but after a year, Sue is still seeing a lack of commitment and very little follow-through from her when it comes to executing and getting things done. Sue called me to vent. The following is a sampling of our conversation.

Sue: Theresa, I sat down with my employee, just as you recommended, and I had a talk with her. I told her I was not pleased with how things have been going lately. Although she is doing some things well to help me with my marketing activities in the office; she just isn't performing the way I expect her to. We've had this same conversation many times. I'm tired of the excuses. She complains to my other employees about how unhappy she is in her job! I like her as a person, but I think she is really holding us back as a team.

Theresa: I'm sure that is frustrating. It sounds like you've given her a lot of time to turn things around, and she's not improving. I know you meet weekly with your team to make sure everyone understands your goals and what's required, and I know you have spent a lot of time training her. What do you think is holding her back?

Sue: I don't think she is committed to this job—or to me. My lead salesperson asked me the other day why this employee is even still working here. She isn't doing her job, and it's obvious to everyone that she isn't committed to us as a team.

Theresa: Sue, I think you know what you need to do with this employee. But there is one question you know I need to ask you. (I always ask my clients this question when they seem to be "stuck.") What does your business need from you right now, Sue?

Sue: Well, the business needs me to be the leader and let this employee go. This isn't a good fit for her. I need to tell her our business relationship isn't working and either reduce her hours substantially so she just does marketing-only activities, or help her transition out of my business altogether. I need a strong salesperson at that desk. That's not her.

Sue ultimately helped her employee to leave, and the employee found a job outside of Sue's organization that was better suited for her. The initial conversation was a big dose of some straight talk (accountability) about what Sue noticed in her employee, and how it seemed clear that the employee was not committed. The breakthrough came when Sue neither judged nor blamed her employee for falling short, but rather "noticed" her behavior. I think this approach helped her employee to "come clean" and openly admit that this wasn't the job for her—but that she felt "stuck," unsure how to make a change.

Sue needed to be directive, be the boss, and help her employee to transition out. And when she did so, she was able to free up space for a new employee to step in with renewed energy and commitment.

Sue was able to figure out what her business needed from her once she asked herself an important question. Now ask yourself: What does MY business need from ME?

Being a strong leader requires taking a bold stand for your business. It requires making tough decisions sometimes, and it takes fierce courage to do what's best for everyone on the team. It requires accountability on your part, which includes tapping into your inner wisdom and leading with conviction, even when you have to make unpopular decisions.

Maybe I'm just lucky, but my clients are so nice! They are kind, thoughtful, fun, and often very passionate business owners and team leaders! But sometimes they choose to dream about the goodness in their people and be perceived as nice so they give their employees many, many—too many—chances to do what they signed up to do! And when their team members fall short of executing their action plans, they begin to justify "why" their team members aren't doing what they are supposed to do. THIS IS CRAZY!!

The problem is, sometimes being "nice" is not productive.

If you, as Leader, set out to do something, you DO it! If you don't get it done, you at least change the course and renegotiate the terms to achieve your goals. Why would you expect any less from anyone who works on your team?

THE ROWERS' CODE

I recently learned to row. Little did I know that rowing is the most challenging sport to master as a team; absolute interdependence is required from everyone on the team if you want to win. Amazing precision and skill are needed from every team member, with nothing short of 100 percent execution from everyone *at the same time* in order to move the boat with excellence.

At a workshop I helped to facilitate with Marilyn Krichko, founder of The Rowers' Code and author of the book of the same name[1], I had the opportunity to row with a team of Microsoft employees who were learning about teambuilding and how rowing can help to transform a team's productivity. I was amazed to witness a table of eight virtual strangers from varying project work groups take a few powerful concepts and create team synergy by simple setting an intention of commitment.

During the workshop, our rowing coach, Charles, said something that really hit home with me. He said, "In rowing, it takes eight people to win a race. It only takes one to lose."

And isn't that what sums it up for just about any team?

If everyone on the team is committed, and everyone is honoring the business' needs, nothing but an outstanding opportunity for results can exist. And when we don't honor the business' needs when it comes to our people, our systems and processes, our business strategies, and our leadership, we are left with mediocre results.

---

1 For more information, visit http://www.rowerscode.com/index.php

THE WISDOM OF KNOWING WHAT YOUR BUSINESS NEEDS

So how do you know what it is that your business needs? Let's find out!

The reality is, sometimes leaders are simply in denial. It's easy to state the organization's strengths fairly well, but when it comes to identifying the weaknesses, that's not so easy.

In the next few pages, we are going to take the old SWOT analysis (**Strengths, Weaknesses, Opportunities, and Threats**) and break it down with simplicity. We are going to focus on two vital questions that I ask all potential clients when trying to assess how I can help them:

1. What is working really well in your organization right now?

2. Where do you get "stuck"?

Step One:

In the space provided, list at least a dozen things you do really well as a business team. These can be as specific or as broad as you wish. Some examples might be:

- "My team is excellent at communicating. We meet daily to discuss strategies, let each other know where we need support, and strategize together to solve problems."

- "Our clients count on us to know them by name when they come into our office."

- "We are consistently on target for reaching our production goals."

1. _____

2. _____

3. _____

4. _____

5. _____

6. _____

7. _____

8. _____

9. _____

10._____

11._____

12._____

Step Two:

In the space provided, list at least twelve areas where you and your team get "stuck." What are those things that hold you back from achieving goals? What gets in the way of you achieving excellence as a team? Some examples might be:

- "My team wastes time in meetings. We tend to meet regularly, but there is never an agenda and it seems like we end up complaining about problems rather than creating solutions when we get together to talk."

- "Our customer service ratings have declined in recent years. People are leaving because of price and they don't see the value in our relationship when we serve them."

- "Our overall production is down. Some months we do okay, but many months we don't achieve our goals. We are inconsistent in our results."

1. _____

2. _____

3. _____

4. _____

5. _____

6. _____

7. _____

8. _____

9. _____

10. _____

11. _____

12. _____

HONOR THE BUSINESS

This exercise should help to affirm the good stuff—what your business and your team is doing well to achieve results. Taking pause to recognize what is working well allows for intentional focus on keeping things moving in the right direction! It also creates an opportunity to provide feedback for everyone about the positive things that are happening as you learn and grow. It can take years to create a rich list of accomplishments and areas where you have great team synergy and success, so don't take those things for granted. Honor them and make sure to take inventory regularly of what is working well so you can ensure that you stay on track. This is a fun and positive opportunity to strengthen team alliance and renew commitment from everyone. Let it inspire you!

The objective behind this exercise is also to shine the light on the areas that are holding you back. We all get "stuck." We all fall short of expectations sometimes, and it's easy to feel as if the business were running us, rather than us running the business. It's that whirlwind of chaos that Stephen Covey so brilliantly speaks of, when we can't seem to move forward and sometimes we don't even know how.

When we know where we are "stuck" and begin the discovery process of identifying why we are stuck, we can begin to shift things. By asking the questions, "What does the business need from me? From my team?" you can begin putting strategies in place for making change. By honoring the business' needs, you also allow for a subjective approach to the decision-making process.

The example I used in the beginning of this chapter with my client is a perfect example of allowing yourself, as business leader, not to carry the burden of always figuring things out on your own. Taking a step back, and making decisions from a broader place, the view from above, will allow you to tap into your business leader wisdom as a resource for making tough decisions about the business' needs. In Sue's case, this isn't about being "nice" or doing what she "wants" to achieve a certain outcome. It's about doing what's right for the business by making strategic business decisions that honor the business' needs. And it's the only way to manage for performance.

CHAPTER FIFTEEN

BREAKING THROUGH BARRIERS FOR INTENTIONAL PRODUCTIVITY

Action is the foundational key to all success.
~ Pablo Picasso

I often ask my clients, "Describe what a 'good day' means to you. What makes a day a really good day?" The number one response I get from my clients and their team members is:

"A good day is a day when I had a list of things to do, and I got everything on my list done! I met my goals and I was able to go home at a reasonable hour feeling like I'd done what I needed to do that day. That makes for a really good day."

I call that a day of intentional productivity. You set out to do something, and you had the time and freedom to do it.

I selected the tag line "Intentional Productivity" for my business with, well, intention! Having clear objectives established for your time and then executing through your actions has a powerful effect on your overall wellbeing. One definitive fact we all are faced with is that there are only a certain number of minutes in our day. If we are going to show up at work or tackle any task, the only way we are going to achieve results is if we set about the business of identifying the intention behind why we are doing what we are doing.

In a team environment, identifying this intention is especially important. Rather than showing up and reacting to everything that is going on around us, it's vital to have clear objectives for your time.

But what happens when we get "stuck"?

In Chapter 6, I mentioned Kathy Kolbe, Founder and Chairwoman of the Kolbe Corp, and how, for over thirty years, she has been studying conation to determine why we do what we do. When asked how she handles getting stuck, Kathy's response was:

> "When nothing works, do nothing."

By that, I think she means: Often we get "stuck" in a reactive state—simply responding to everything that is going on around us, rather than approaching the problem-solving phase with intention. For some of us, it feels like a luxury when we can work with such intention! But here's the deal: Simply reacting, staying "stuck" in that whirlwind, usually doesn't allow us to move forward effectively. And when we are trying to be productive, and execute a plan, we need to follow our instinct and act with intention.

When researching what it is that gets us "unstuck," so we can break through barriers that are holding us back, some common themes surfaced. The #1 response from all who responded to the question, "What gets you 'unstuck' when you are stuck and can't move forward?" was:

> "Act. Do something. Anything."

We've all heard stories of the proverbial mouse, running fast in its cage and getting nowhere fast. Sometimes we find ourselves running so fast from one thing to the next that we forget what it is we are chasing! But one thing is certain: Doing nothing allows us to stop, take inventory, and ask, "What's trying to happen here?" Without asking this question, we end up continuing to react to those things around us, and expending mental and physical energy that depletes us. If we want to move forward, we have to step off of the wheel in the cage and do something different. We have to act.

One of the most difficult things I have had to learn to say as a leader, a mother, and as a coach is, "I don't know." I'm great at guessing or brainstorming possibilities, but without guidance, collaboration, and seeking to find the truth, I'm left with only my story and the lens that I wake up and see through every day. My story and lens have their limitations, and if I only relied on my own perspective all the time, I know I would hold myself back (and everyone else).

Most leaders, I find, rely on their peers to help move them forward when they are stuck. There is a reason great leaders are drawn to other great leaders—it's because we want to learn and grow and gain support from them to move us forward. Breaking through barriers is not something we want to do alone, so working with others allows us the creative forces to problem-solve outside the box.

Joe Williams, a colleague through my work as a Kolbe Certified™ Consultant and a Rocket Scientist from NASA, explained to me his process for breaking through barriers and getting "unstuck":

NASA's human spaceflight future is turbulent and cloudy, with lots of obstacles in the way that impede change. What do I do when I get stuck? I play to my strengths and get as diverse of a problem-solving team as I can get. My strength is experimentation—try something, anything, to move forward. Others are great planners, so developing and sticking to a plan is a way to overcome barriers.

I think Joe has learned the power of tapping into his own talent, taking action, and collaborating with others. Leadership can create a feeling of isolation at the top, so creating opportunities to work with others to improve results is inspiring, motivating, and helps us to feel supported when making change is necessary.

THE POWER OF COLLABORATION

Collaboration is something you can model for your team. A "think tank," brainstorming session, or an off-site day of planning is one of the easiest ways to call your team forward to begin the process of shifting the stall.

In order to make change and create action, the entire team must be in alignment. I have found a process that can be effective for any working group. I call it the Systems-Based Solution for putting strategy in place for success. If you want to plan an on-site meeting or you have the luxury of getting your team off-site for a full day or even a half-day, that is my recommendation, but you can also take components of this system and break them down into mini-meetings over a short period of time for great effectiveness.

THE SYSTEMS-BASED SOLUTION—DESIGNING AN EFFECTIVE OFF-SITE PLANNING SESSION:

1. Conduct a culture audit on your organization by finding out from all the players at every level what's working and where the team feels stuck. (Refer to Chapter 12 for a sample of a simple culture audit.) Make sure that all voices are heard. Remember that Deep Democracy is the only way the system can be truly honored. Feedback and input from everyone ensures you haven't missed any important issues that need to be resolved.

2. Hire a facilitator, coach, or mentor to analyze the feedback with you to determine what steps should be taken to work through the information. The key here is in the collaborative support that a working business partner can offer you so you don't have to make decisions alone.

3. Participate with your team. I find that when I facilitate planning meetings for my clients, I like the leader to be on a level playing field with the rest of the team so they can participate fully. This creates alignment for everyone on the team and allows the leader to be with the team in the trenches. The value arrives in the insights you can gain as leader, and the full accessibility you can provide to your team. It's important for your team members to see that you can roll up your sleeves and get the work done *with* them, not for them.

4. Customize the meeting to fit the business' needs. The information from the culture audit will provide almost everything you need to know about how your team sees things—what's working well allows for a chance to celebrate your success. We forget how im-

portant this part of team development is. And putting the tough issues on the table for discussion allows for you, as leader, to tackle the not-so-pretty issues in a non-threatening way. Of course we get stuck. So what are we going to do about it? Burying our heads in the sand has proven to be ineffective. So let's get after it.

5. Set yourselves up in a safe place, in a meeting room with a u-shaped desk. This arrangement is vital for good communication and collaboration. Everyone needs to see the facilitator and have easy access to one another.

6. Make sure you focus on high-touch and low-tech. What I'm getting at here is an opportunity to put the laptops away, keep the PowerPoints to a minimum, and go crazy with blank sheets of paper. The best sessions I have facilitated have included flipcharts with colorful markers throughout the room, notepads and pencils in front of everyone, and activities that allow everyone to get up and move around throughout the day. This stipulation isn't about how to present to the team. It's about the human element of communication and sharing by engaging the team to step up and step into a powerful day of learning and developing.

7. Assign someone to be present to record the entire day. You can have the event videotaped, or simply have someone take notes by capturing all the information that is co-created throughout the day. Recording the information is vital for you as team leader for follow-up and integration following the meeting. Otherwise, key elements can get lost, and this information is more valuable than anything else you will obtain throughout the year.

8. Always, always leave a few minutes at the day's end for all participants to provide feedback on the day. This evaluation process should be simple and allow each participant to report what he or she learned, what changes he would implement, what concerns he has moving forward, and what general feedback he would like to provide you, as leader, about his experience that day. This feedback also should be optionally confidential. This vital information provides immediate feedback to you about the effectiveness of the day, from the team's perspective.

9. Send a written recap to all participants following the meeting that includes the day's key elements. Include action plans that were developed, notes from meeting discussions, and any information that needs to be distributed. For those who were assigned follow-up tasks, these re-cap notes are a wonderful gift. Make sure the notes arrive in everyone's email inbox within three business days following the event. In the recap, make sure there is an action plan for carrying forward and executing your plan.

10. Execute. Establish a system for following up on all of the powerful work that was done during the day of planning. Too often, I see teams go back to the office following an off-site planning meeting only to become distracted by the day-to-day tasks of getting things done. All of the dynamic, strategic planning that was created at the planning meeting gets lost in someone's office corner, flipcharts stay rolled up, and Action Plans become a dream not realized! What a terrible shame. Make sure a plan is in place for carrying out your plan before the planning meeting ends so it is easier to execute.

11. Track your progress quarterly. Ask everyone to take ownership of carrying out specific tasks and allow the team members to create strategic work groups to create solutions and implement necessary plans. Measuring progress allows for increased ownership and accountability at every level. Again, you don't have to do everything alone.

Empower your team members by calling them forward in a new way. Honor the system. Leading doesn't mean you have to do it all yourself. But it is up to you to create space for them to step up and step in by taking ownership and creating outcomes for success. It's about setting intentions as a team, and using those opportunities when you are feeling "stuck" to work together to create solutions.

Being productive means following through. Even the simplest of goals don't mean anything if nobody takes them seriously. Poor execution is almost always a result of not following through.

Let this be the year you break through with great intention and achieve all that you dream of. Step into it boldly and know that your team is counting on you to get it right. And so are you.

RESOURCES

Personal Mission Statement

- What would I really like to be and do in my life?

- What do I feel are my greatest strengths?

- How do I want to be remembered?

- Who is the one person who has made the greatest positive impact in my life?

- What have been my happiest moments in life?

- If I had unlimited time and resources, what would I do?

- What are the three or four most important things to me?

- How can I best contribute to the world?

❋ Team Synergy Institute
INTENTIONAL PRODUCTIVITY

Theresa Callahan, Executive and Team Development Coach
www.teamsynergyinstitute.com

Entrepreneur/Leadership Wheel

Directions: Score (0 to 10) your satisfaction with your ability to:

Planning and Budgeting: establishing detailed steps and timetables for achieving results and then allocating the resources necessary to make it happen

Establishing Direction: developing a vision of the future, often the distant future, and strategies for producing the changes needed to achieve that vision

Organizing and Staffing: establishing a structure for accomplishing plan requirements, staffing that structure with people, delegating authority for carrying out the plan, providing policies and procedures to guide people, and creating methods of systems to monitor implementation

Aligning People: communicating the direction by words and deeds to all those whose cooperation may be needed so as to create a team that understands the vision and strategies and accepts their validity

Controlling and Problem Solving: monitoring results in detail, indentifying deviation from the plan, and then organizing to solve these problems

Motivating and Inspiring: energizing people to overcome major political, bureaucratic, and resource barriers to change by satisfying basic, but often unfulfilled, human needs

Promoting Stability and Order: creating the potential of consistently producing key results

Promoting Change: creating the potential of producing useful change (such as desired new products)[1]

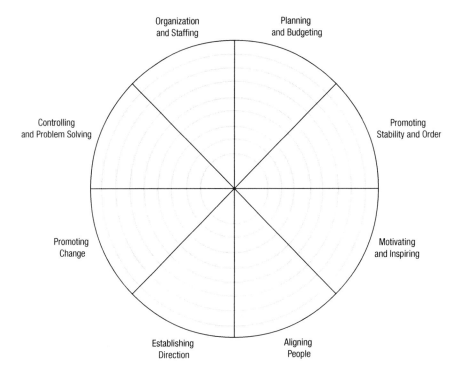

LEADERSHIP WHEEL

The eight sections of the Wheel represent Balance. Seeing the center of the wheel as 0 and the outer edges at 10, <u>rank your level of satisfaction</u> with each area by drawing a straight or curved line to create a new outer edge. The new perimeter represents the wheel of your life as the Entrepreneur and Leader of your business. If this were a real wheel, how bumpy would the ride be?

---

1 Refer to thecoaches.com for updated assessment tools and resources.

Primary Focus

Name: _____

Once you have ranked your level of satisfaction in the areas indicated on the Leadership Wheel, you are ready to select three focus areas as a framework for setting goals, designing projects and making commitments to change.

In the space below and on the next page, name and describe the three areas you would like to hold as the primary focus of your leadership development. For each area, provide a simple heading and a sense of where you currently are feeling "stuck".

EXAMPLE: _Planning and Budgeting_

"I have been running my business for almost 8 years now, and I am tired of feeling like my overhead is out of control. I don't want to continue relying on my line of credit and personal assets to pay my bills at work – I want my business to pay for itself."

1. _____

_____

_____

_____

_____

_____

_____

2. _____

_____

_____

_____

_____

_____

_____

_____

_____

3. _____

_____

_____

_____

_____

_____

_____

_____

_____

What would it look like if it were a "10"?

For each item that you wrote down as a primary area of focus, I'd like you describe what it would look like if it were a "10." In other words, what has to happen to reach that pinnacle of success where you know that your goals have been met?

For example, if you ranked yourself a "3" in the area of "Planning and Budgeting," I'd like you to describe what a "10" would look like.

Example:

A "10" in Planning and Budgeting will require:

Having a budget in place that allows me to prioritize spending and saving for the bottom line.

Knowing what my overhead is and honoring my budget on a monthly basis.

Making sure the bills are paid on a timely basis and that forecasting is seamless.

Having a marketing budget in place that is in alignment with our production goals.

1. A "10" in _____ will require:

- _____

- _____

- _____

- _____

2. A "10" in _____ will require:

- _____

- _____

- _____

- _____

3. A "10" in _____ will require:

- _____

- _____

- _____

- _____

Goal Planning Worksheet

Goal #1

Determine the timeframe: quarterly, yearly

Goal #1 _____

Special skills/knowledge/strengths I can use to reach this goal:

_____

_____

_____

_____

_____

What motivation do I have to accomplish this goal?

_____

_____

_____

_____

_____

Steps to achieve this goal:

- _____

- _____

- _____

- _____

How will I know when I have achieved this goal? (What accountability measures are in place to track results?)

_____

_____

_____

_____

Goal #2

Determine the timeframe: quarterly, yearly

Goal #2 _____

Special skills/knowledge/strengths I can use to reach this goal:

_____

_____

_____

_____

What motivation do I have to accomplish this goal?

_____

_____

_____

_____

Steps to achieve this goal:

- _____

- _____

- _____

- _____

How will I know when I have achieved this goal? (What accountability measures are in place to track results?)

_____

_____

_____

_____

Goal #3

Determine the timeframe: quarterly, yearly

Goal #3 _____

Special skills/knowledge/strengths I can use to reach this goal:

_____

_____

_____

_____

What motivation do I have to accomplish this goal?

_____

_____

_____

_____

Steps to achieve this goal:

- _____

- _____

- _____

- _____

How will I know when I have achieved this goal? (What accountability measures are in place to track results?)

_____

_____

_____

_____

Team Culture Audit

Feedback from these questions will help to shine the light on what is truly going on within the organization and help to identify areas of team synergy as well as areas of strain or conflict among the team players. The collective feedback from this process will immediately help the team leader to understand why the team is "stuck" and begin putting a plan in place for teambuilding, heightened awareness and solutions for creating a stronger team alliance.

1. I have a clear job description and know what my job duties are?
Yes   No

Please explain:

_____

_____

_____

_____

2. I am provided with job training that allows me to do my job better and with more ease:

Never   Rarely   Sometimes   Almost Always   Always

Please explain:

_____

_____

_____

_____

3. I feel driven to make a difference in my organization:

Never   Rarely   Sometimes   Almost Always   Always

Please explain:

_____

_____

_____

_____

4. In your opinion, what inspires people to make a difference in the organization?

_____

_____

_____

_____

My organization recognizes and celebrates successes of team members:

Never   Rarely   Sometimes   Almost Always   Always

Please explain:

_____

_____

_____

_____

5. How could your team improve the way it recognizes the successes of individual team members?

_____

_____

_____

_____

6. We work together as a team:

Never   Rarely   Sometimes   Almost Always   Always

Please explain:

_____

_____

_____

_____

7. What do you believe are important characteristics of a good team?

_____

_____

_____

_____

8. My organization communicates effectively (written and verbal) and in a timely manner to its employees:

Never   Rarely   Sometimes   Almost Always   Always

Please explain:

_____

_____

_____

_____

9. I enjoy starting a new day:

Never   Rarely   Sometimes   Almost Always   Always

Please explain:

_____

_____

_____

_____

10. What makes a really good day for you?

_____

_____

_____

_____

11. Describe what makes your organization great and what could make it better?

_____

_____

_____

_____

12. What does your organization need to be focused on to be successful for the next year?

_____

_____

_____

_____

13. If you could implement any change within your organization, what would it be?

_____

_____

_____

_____

Employee Performance Review

Employee Name:	Employee ID:
Job Title:	Date:
Department:	
Manager:	
Review Period:	to:

At least one week prior to this review, notify employee of the review, and assign the employee a self-review as well as an employee peer review.

All goals should be reasonable and specific.

Briefly describe the goals of the employee. Were the goals achieved? If no, then why not?

Goal #1:

Goal #2:

Goal #3:

Use this rating key for the following evaluation:

1= **Unsatisfactory**
   Does not perform required tasks. Requires constant supervision

2= **Marginal**
   Needs improvement in quality of work. Completes tasks, but not on time.

3= **Meets Requirements**
   Meets basic requirements. Tasks are completed on time.

4= **Exceeds Requirements**
   Goes above and beyond expectations.

5= **Exceptional**
   Always gets results far beyond what is required.

	5	4	3	2	1
Achieves Set Objectives	☐	☐	☐	☐	☐
Open to Constructive Criticism	☐	☐	☐	☐	☐
Demonstrates Effective Management and Leadership Skills	☐	☐	☐	☐	☐
Completes All Assigned Responsibilities	☐	☐	☐	☐	☐
Meets Attendance Requirements	☐	☐	☐	☐	☐
Takes Responsibility	☐	☐	☐	☐	☐
Recognize Potential Problems and Develops Solutions	☐	☐	☐	☐	☐
Demonstrates Problem Solving	☐	☐	☐	☐	☐
Offers Constructive Suggestions for Improvement	☐	☐	☐	☐	☐
Generates Creative Ideas and Solutions	☐	☐	☐	☐	☐
Provides Alternatives When Making Recommendations	☐	☐	☐	☐	☐

Additional Comments:

Provide Suggestions for Self-Improvement:

Supervisor/Manager Feedback:

Verification of Review

By signing this form, you confirm that you have discussed this review in detail with your supervisor. Signing this form does not necessarily indicate that you agree with this evaluation.

I, _____ acknowledge receipt of review, and my signature does not necessarily indicate agreement.

Employee Signature:

Manager Signature:

Business Team Checkup – simplifying the SWOT analysis

In this exercise, we are going to take the old SWOT analysis (Strengths, Weaknesses, Opportunities, and Threats) and break it down with simplicity by focusing on two vital questions

What is working really well in your organization right now?

Where do you get "stuck"?

<u>Step One</u>:

In the space provided, list at least a dozen things you do really well as a business team. These can be as specific or as broad as you wish. Some examples might be:

- "My team is excellent at communicating. We meet daily to discuss strategies, let each other know where we need support, and strategize together to solve problems."

- "Our clients count on us to know them by name when they come into our office."

- "We are consistently on target for reaching our production goals."

1. _____

2. _____

3. _____

4. _____

5. _____

6. _____

7. _____

8. _____

9. _____

10._____

11._____

12._____

<u>Step Two</u>:

In the space provided, list at least twelve areas where you and your team get "stuck." What are those things that hold you back from achieving goals? What gets in the way of you achieving excellence as a team? Some examples might be:

- "My team wastes time in meetings. We tend to meet regularly, but there is never an agenda and it seems like we end up complaining about problems rather than creating solutions when we get together to talk."

- "Our customer service ratings have declined in recent years. People are leaving because of price and they don't see the value in our relationship when we serve them."

- "Our overall production is down. Some months we do okay, but many months we don't achieve our goals. We are inconsistent in our results."

1. _____

2. _____

3. _____

4. _____

5. _____

6. _____

7. _____

8. _____

9. _____

10._____

11._____

12._____

Professional Development Action Plan

Professional development, also known as continuing education, should be an essential component of your career growth and plan. With constant change and the evolution of our business needs, keeping your skills and knowledge current will give you a competitive advantage in achieving your career goals. As with your other life goals, it is recommended that you develop a personalized action plan designed to help you achieve your goals. A plan with explicit goals will provide structure for your future learning. Life-long learning is the key to growth and empowerment.

Based upon your personal assessment of your current knowledge, skills and abilities, or based upon your results from assessment tools we have used and feedback you have received from others, ask yourself the following questions:

- How can I improve or strengthen my work performance?

- What are the key areas I want or need to develop to remain proficient in my profession?

- What are new skills and knowledge I will need in the future?

After determining the key learning areas in which you want to focus, develop specific and measurable goals in which to pursue. Use this template to facilitate your goal-setting process, to document your results, and to track your accomplishments.

Professional Development
Action Plan Worksheet

As I develop my Action Plan, I will use the SMART model by ensuring all of my goals and action steps are **S**pecific, **M**easurable, **A**ttainable, **R**ealistic and within a specific **T**imeframe. Complete a plan for each of my goals.

Name: _____ **Date:** _____

Goal: _____

Relevance – how will this goal help me:

_____

_____

_____

_____

_____

What are the steps or strategies I will take?	What is the realistic timeframe to accomplish the step or strategy?	How will I evaluate each step or strategy?	How will I know the step or strategy has been accomplished?

Sample – Professional Development Action Plan

As I develop my Action Plan, I will use the SMART model by ensuring all of my goals and action steps are **S**pecific, **M**easurable, **A**ttainable, **R**ealistic and within a specific **T**imeframe. Complete a plan for each of my goals.

Goal: Develop my presentation (public-speaking) skills

Relevance – how will this goal help me: My current job requires me to occasionally give oral presentations to internal and external clients. By gaining competency and proficiency in this area, I will build my confident, which will result in more effective and persuasive communication with positive outcomes and reduce my anxiety when called upon to speak publicly.

What are the steps or strategies I will take?	What is the realistic timeframe to accomplish the step or strategy?	How will I evaluate each step or strategy?	How will I know the step or strategy has been accomplished?
Take a public workshop on presentation skills.	Complete the workshop within six months.	After the workshop, I will test my knowledge in the fundamentals of public speaking.	Upon course completion.
Read at least two intermediate-level books on presentation skills.	By July 1st.	After reading the books, I will measure my knowledge on more advanced presentation techniques.	The two books identified will have been informative and helpful in educating me on more advanced presentation skills.
Join Toastmasters International to frequently practice my newly acquired presentation skills.	Join within the next three months; participate in weekly meetings for at least six months.	I will measure progress by soliciting feedback from other Toastmaster participates; pursue certification.	Through frequent practice, my skill level should improve. At a minimum, I will become more proficient in preparing for presentations and reducing anxiety.
Seek out new opportunities to present information and reports in a team setting.	Immediately.	I will measure progress by soliciting feedback from team members and my manager.	By giving at least one oral presentation per month at staff meetings.

.

RECOMMENDED READING

Ben-Shahar, Tal. *Happier: Learn the Secrets to Daily Joy and Lasting Fulfillment.* New York: McGraw-Hill, 2007.

Bossidy, Larry, Ram Charan and Charles Burck. *Execution: The Discipline of Getting Things Done.* New York: Crown Business, 2002.

Carson, Rick. *Taming Your Gremlin: A Surprisingly Simple Method for Getting Out of Your Own Way.* New York: HarperCollins, 2003.

Covey, Stephen R. *The 4 Disciplines of Execution: The Secrets to Getting Things Done, on Time, With Excellence.* Salt Lake City, UT: Franklin Covey, 2008.

Demos, Mark. *Who R U? LSI: The Forensics of Purpose, Passion and Performance.* n.p.: 2011.

Kimsey-House, Henry, Karen Kimsey-House and Phillip Sandahl. *Co-Active Coaching: Changing Business, Transforming Lives.* Boston, MA: Nicholas Brealey Publishing, 2011.

Kolbe, Kathy. *Pure Instinct: The M.O. of High Performance People and Teams.* Phoenix, AZ: Monument Press, 2004

Krichko, Marilyn with Jane Rollinson. *The Rowers' Code: A Business Parable of How to Pull Together as a Team—and Win!* Pompton Plains, NJ: Career Press, 2011.

Lencioni, Patrick. *The Five Dysfunctions of a Team: A Leadership Fable.* San Francisco, CA: Jossey-Bass, 2002.

Rath, Tom and Barrie Conchie. *Strengths Based Leadership.* New York: Gallup Press, 2008.

Rath, Tom and Jim Harter. *Wellbeing: The Five Essential Elements.* New York: Gallup Press, 2010.

ABOUT TEAM SYNERGY INSTITUTE

Team Synergy Institute is based in Seattle, Washington, and led by Executive and Team Development Coach, Theresa Callahan. Theresa has clients throughout the country and conducts on-site coaching and facilitation at her clients' locations as well as one-on-one and team training via phone conference calls and tele-workshops.

Theresa and her team provide Leadership and Team Development coaching to business owners and team leaders within organizations, as well as business teams of all sizes.

In addition to one-on-one coaching with her clients and team members, Theresa creates customized team training and business planning events for small teams and large organizations.

The philosophies that drive results for the organization are centered around team talent and making sure the right people are in the right jobs for increased performance and improved job satisfaction for everyone on the team, including the team leader. Theresa believes that the key ingredient to team success is matching the talent with the job and providing strong leadership that includes accountability measures to ensure the team can thrive.

The clients that Theresa and her team partner with express improved results and increased efficiencies with the systems and processes that are implemented as a result of their partnership and collaborative approach to running the business.

Theresa offers key-note speaking events for small and large events, focusing on key elements for building a high performance team and increasing effectiveness as a team leader.

Theresa's training includes high-impact coaching strategies from the Coaches Training Institute and the Center for Right Relationship.

ABOUT TEAM SYNERGY RECRUITING

Team Synergy Recruiting is a division of Theresa Callahan's coaching and consulting company, Team Synergy Institute.

Theresa has two assistants who work with her to find team talent for her clients in the insurance and financial services industry. Theresa's hand-on approach to this process was launched in 2011 and she is having great success helping her clients ensure job fit for team talent candidates.

Theresa believes that your talent is the engine that drives your business productivity. She invites her clients to partner with her to find the talent that fits the needs of their business.

Team Synergy Recruiting provides clients with:

- A pool of top candidates to interview

- A customized HR tool-kit that includes:

  - A strategic Interview Guide tailored for the position

  - Templates for creating job descriptions & professional development plans

- A 30-, 60-, 90-day review process

- Coaching and support facilitating talent-based assessment tools that will help to identify talent that "fits" the roles and responsibilities of the job

- A <u>90-day guaranteed replacement</u> for new hires that don't work out

For information call Theresa Callahan

425-241-4855